Progressive

W9-AVS-677

LEAD GUITAR

by
Gary Turner & Brenton White

Visit our Website
www.learntoplaymusic.com

The Progressive Series of Music Instruction Books, CDs, and DVDs

PROGRESSIVE LEAD GUITAR
I.S.B.N. 0 969540 46 6
Order Code: CP-54046

Acknowledgments
Photographs: Phil Martin

For more information on this series contact;
L.T.P. Publishing Pty Ltd
email: info@learntoplaymusic.com
or visit our website;
www.learntoplaymusic.com

COPYRIGHT CONDITIONS
No part of this product can be reproduced in any
form without the written consent of the publishers.
© 2003 L.T.P. Publishing Pty Ltd

LIST OF CONTENTS

INTRODUCTION

The lead guitarist is generally considered to be the most important instrumentalist in a rock/pop group. A group's 'sound' and direction will be influenced by his or her ability and style.

Progressive Lead Guitar will provide you with an essential guide into the scales and techniques used by lead guitarists. Within the three main sections of this book, a lesson by lesson structure has been used to give a clear and carefully graded method of study.

Progressive Lead Guitar is designed to teach beginning lead guitarists, but not beginning guitarists. Before the commencement of this text your knowledge should include:

1. Open and bar chords, particularly root 6 (E formation) and root 5 (A formation) bar chord shapes*.

2. Basic music theory.

Development in these areas should continue in conjunction with the study of lead guitar.

Combine the study of this book with constant playing and listening. All rock/pop lead guitarists use the same basic scales and techniques, but the development of style is determined by how these basics are used.

*See *Progressive Rhythm Guitar* by Gary Turner and Brenton White.

Using the Compact Disc

It is recommended that you have a copy of the accompanying compact disc that includes all the examples in this book. The book shows you where to put your fingers and what technique to use and the recording lets you hear how each example should sound. Practice the examples slowly at first, gradually increasing tempo. Once you are confident you can play the example evenly without stopping the beat, try playing along with the recording. You will hear a drum beat at the beginning of each example, to lead you into the example and to help you keep time. To play along with the CD your guitar must be in tune with it. If you have tuned using an electronic tuner (see below) your guitar will already be in tune with the CD. A small diagram of a compact disc with a number as shown below indicates a recorded example. Many of the tracks on the CD contain more than one example. In these cases, index points are used (1.0, 1.1, 1.2 etc). If your CD player has an index points function, you can select each example individually. If not, each example will automatically follow the previous one. The first track on the CD contains the notes of the six open strings of the guitar. 1.0 is the 6th string (low E)1.1 is the open A string, 1.3 is the open D string, etc.

 1.0 ← CD Track Number

Fretboard Diagrams

Fretboard diagrams are given throughout this book to show which patterns and fingerings are given for each scale. To know how to read the diagrams, study the following illustration.

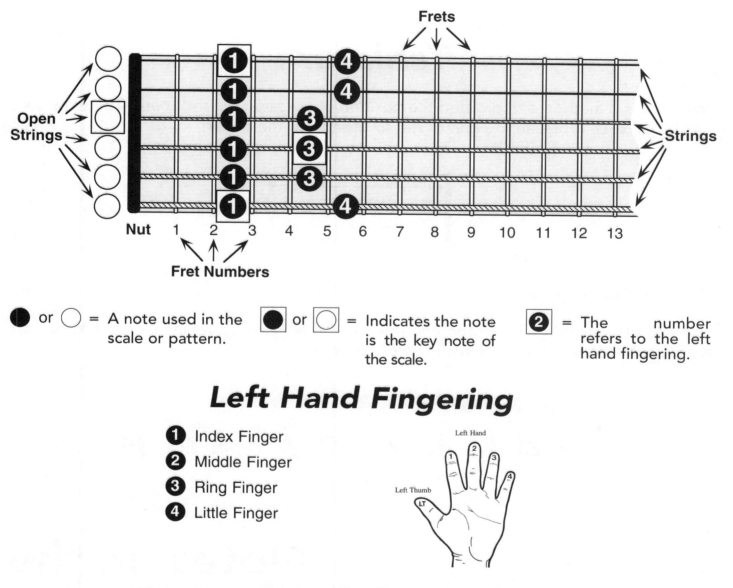

● or ○ = A note used in the scale or pattern.

⬛ or ⬜ = Indicates the note is the key note of the scale.

②| = The   number refers to the left hand fingering.

Left Hand Fingering

❶ Index Finger
❷ Middle Finger
❸ Ring Finger
❹ Little Finger

Tuning Your Guitar to the CD

Before you commence each lesson or practice session you will need to tune your guitar. If your guitar is out of tune everything you play will sound incorrect even though you are holding the correct notes. On the accompanying CD the **first six index points** correspond to the **six strings of the guitar**. For a complete description of how to tune your guitar, see *Progressive Guitar Method 1*.

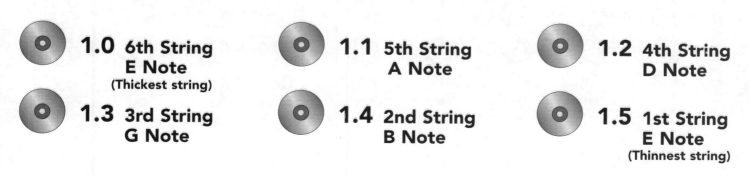

1.0 6th String **E Note** (Thickest string)

1.1 5th String **A Note**

1.2 4th String **D Note**

1.3 3rd String **G Note**

1.4 2nd String **B Note**

1.5 1st String **E Note** (Thinnest string)

6

Notation

Two methods of music notation are presented in this book; namely notes and tablature. You need only use one of these methods*, whichever is most convenient (if you are not familiar with note reading follow the tablature outlined below).

Tablature

Tablature is a method of indicating the position of notes on the fretboard. There are six 'tab' lines, each representing one of the six strings on the guitar:

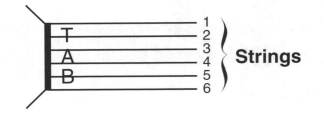

*Note readers may need to refer to the tablature to determine the position of an exercise.

Note names on the guitar fretboard: The musical alphabet contains seven letters, with sharps and flats occurring between five of them as such:

A A#/Bb B C C#/Db D D#/Eb E F F#/Gb G G#/Ab A

Notes on the

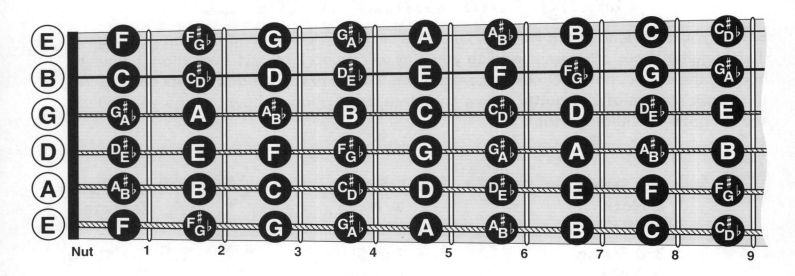

When a number is placed on one of the lines, it indicates the fret location of the note e.g.

```
T────────4──────────
A────────────────────
B────────────────────
```

This indicates the **fourth** fret of the **2nd** string (an **E♭** note).

```
T────────────────────
A────────────────────
B────────7──────────
```

This indicates the **seventh** fret of the **5th** string (an **E** note).

```
T────────────────────
A────────0──────────
B────────────────────
```

This indicates the **3rd** string open (a **G** note).

The tablature, as used in this book, does not indicate the time values of the notes, only their position on the fretboard. You can read the time values by following the count written beneath the tablature, e.g.

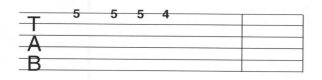

Count: **1**   **2** **+** **3**   4

In this example the 1st note is worth 1 count, the 2nd and 3rd notes are worth $\frac{1}{2}$ a count each and the 4th note is worth 2 counts.

Guitar Fretboard

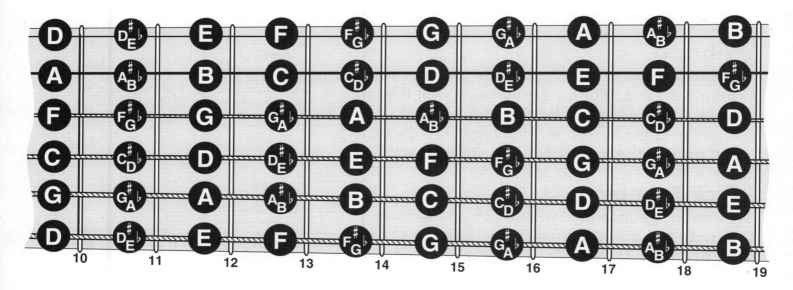

Tablature Symbols

The following tablature symbols will appear throughout this book.

The Hammer-On

A curved line and the letter H indicates a hammer-on. The first note is played but the second note is produced by hammering on the left hand finger, which plays the second note.

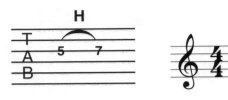

The Pull-Off

A curved line and the letter P indicates a pull-off. The first note is played but the second note is produced by pulling off the left hand finger, which plays the second note.

The Slide

The letter S and a straight line indicates a slide. If the line comes from below the number, slide from a lower fret but if the line is above the number, slide from a higher fret.

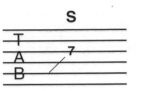

The Bend

The letter B and a curved line represents a bend. The note is played by the left hand finger which bends the string (from the note indicated in the tab to the pitch of the note in brackets).

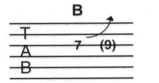

The Release Bend

A curved line on the top left hand side of the number and the letter R indicates a release bend. This technique involves bending the note indicated with the left hand (from the pitch of the note in brackets), playing the string whilst bent, then returning the string to its normal position. The release bend creates a drop in pitch from a higher note to a lower note.

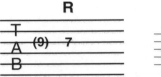

Vibrato

A wavy line shown above the note indicates when vibrato is used. Vibrato is controlled with the left hand finger which is fretting the note. As the finger frets the note, move the finger rapidly back and forth in the direction of the adjacent strings.

Pick Tremolo

Three lines above the tablature or on the stem of a note in standard notation indicates pick tremolo. A pick tremolo is played with the pick and involves a rapid playing of a note with continuous alternating down and up picks.

SECTION 1

LESSON ONE

The 12 Bar Blues Progression

A 12 bar Blues is a progression which repeats every 12 bars. You should become familiar with this pattern of chords by playing it through many times.

12 BAR IN A

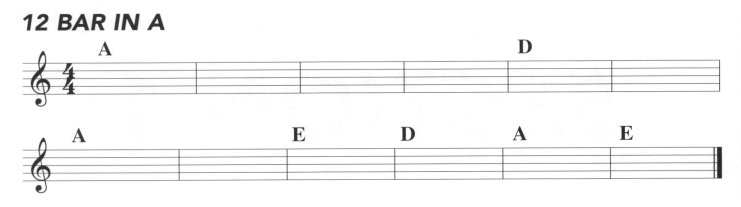

12 Bar Blues Riff Number 1

Lead guitarists often use a technique of playing 'riffs' against the 12 bar Blues. A **riff** is a pattern of notes that is repeated throughout a progression or song. The following example (riff number 1) is played against the 12 bar Blues in the key of A major.

 2.0

For each note of the A chord, this riff starts at the 5th fret of the 6th string. Play this riff slowly and smoothly using a downward motion of the pick, indicated thus: ∨.

Riff One

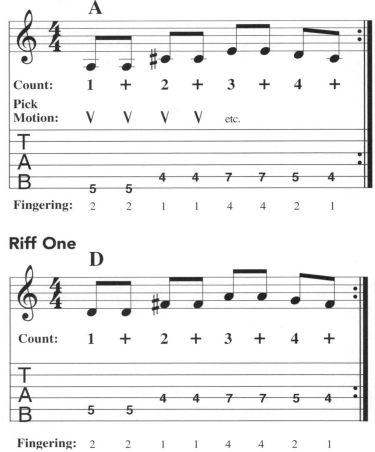

 **2.1**

When the progression changes to a D chord (bar 5), the riff moves across to the 5th string, commencing on the D note (5th fret).

You will notice that the fingering is still the same and that the basic 'shape' of the riff has not altered.

Riff One

2.2

For the E chord (bar 9), the riff shape begins on the 5th string at the 7th fret.

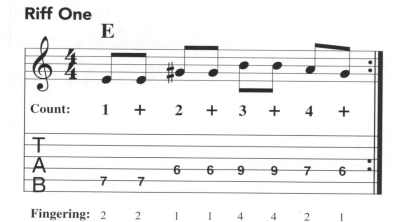

Riff One

 3

Here is the complete 12 bar in A.

Riff One

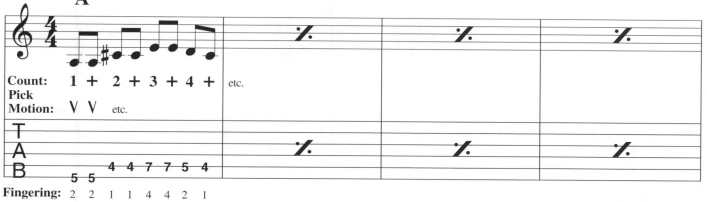

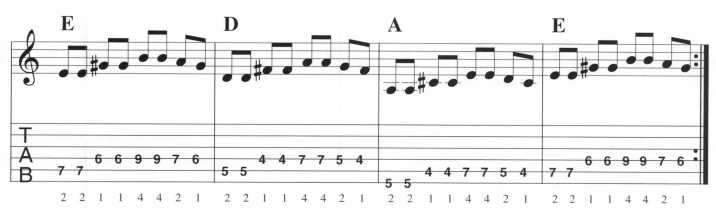

You have probably heard this type of sound before. Play some records (1950's Rock and Roll or Blues songs would be best) and listen for this style of riff playing either by the lead or bass guitarists. Try to make some variations for yourself. Remember that in many old 'Rock & Roll' songs the riff shape is established in the first bar and maintained throughout the song.

LESSON TWO

The Major Scale

The major scale (and scales derived from it) is the basis of most lead guitar playing. For now however, you will only be using it as an exercise for developing left and right hand co-ordination. Written below is a one octave pattern of the A major scale. Observe the correct fingering (finger numbers written inside each note).

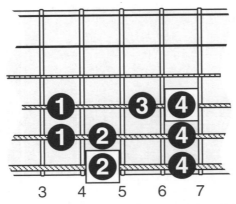

The dots surrounded by a square represent **root** notes. Root notes are notes which have the same name as the scale name, (e.g. A notes are root notes for the A major scale).

🔘 **4.0**

Play through this pattern very slowly, ascending and descending, and you will notice that it has the familiar sound of DO RE MI FA SO LA TI DO. The notes you are playing are written out below.

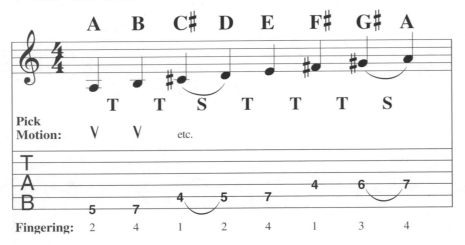

There is only a semitone (1 fret) between the 3rd-4th notes and 7th-8th notes of the major scale (indicated by the curved line). All other notes are separated by a tone (2 frets). The pattern of tones and semitones remains the same for every major scale.

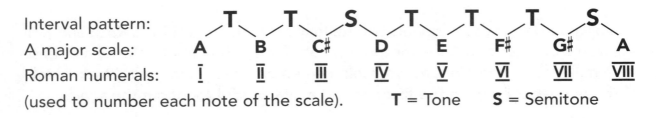

Interval pattern:	T	T	S	T	T	T	S
A major scale:	A	B	C#	D	E	F#	G#	A
Roman numerals:	Ī	ĪĪ	ĪĪĪ	ĪV̄	V̄	V̄Ī	V̄ĪĪ	V̄ĪĪĪ

(used to number each note of the scale).   **T** = Tone   **S** = Semitone

Try the same pattern starting at the 8th fret.

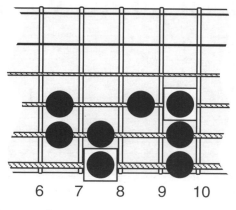

You are now playing a C major scale:

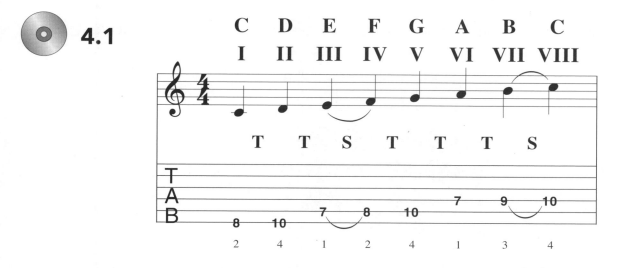

4.1

Notice that it keeps the DO RE MI FA SO LA TI DO sound which was heard with the A major scale. This is because the interval pattern remains the same between each note.

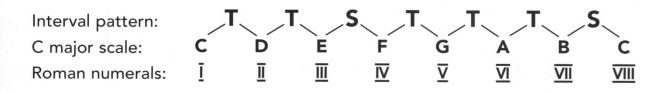

Interval pattern:
C major scale:
Roman numerals:

This major scale pattern can be played by starting at any note on the 6th or 5th strings. The note you start on will be the root note of the scale. E.g. if you start on the 10th fret of the 6th string, you will be playing a D major scale.

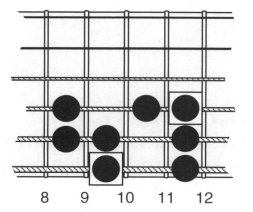

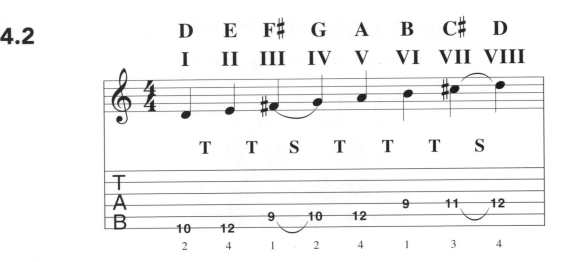

4.2

If you start at the 6th fret of the 5th string, you will be playing an E♭ major scale.

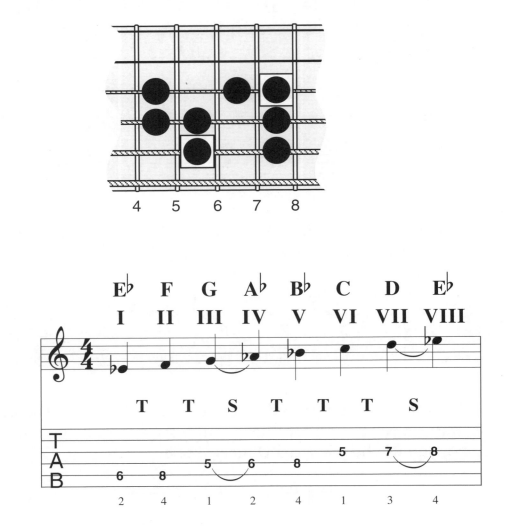

4.3

And so on...

It is probably easiest to relate the scale name to the root 6 (E formation) and root 5 (A formation) bar chord names. Your starting note on the 6th string will have the same name as the root 6 chord for that position; and on the 5th string it will have the same name as the root 5 bar chord for that position.

Left Hand Position

Before you attempt to increase speed in your playing of the major scale, make sure that your left hand is correctly positioned. Each finger should 'line up' with the string being played, and should hover a small distance above it until used. Each finger should also be in line with the four frets being used in the scale. Check your hand position with the photographs below;

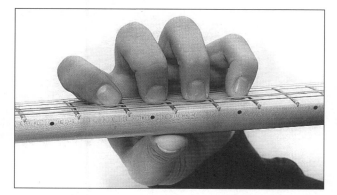 

This hand position will be difficult at first, but is essential if you are to eventually work up to a fast, smooth sound.

Here is an exercise to help you learn the major scale in all keys. Begin by playing the Root 6 (E formation) G major scale both ascending and descending. Then move to the Root 5 (A formation) C major scale. The next step is to move up one fret and repeat the two patterns in the keys of A♭ major and D♭ major. If you keep progressing up the fretboard, it doesn't take long until you have covered all possible keys. It is a good idea to say the name of each key as you play the scale.

 5

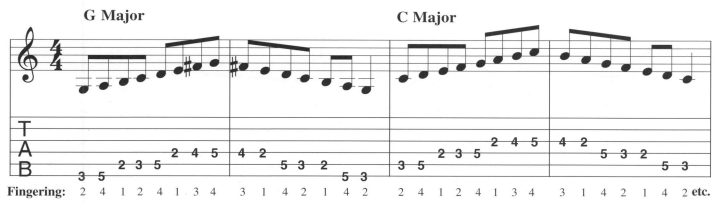

Fingering: 2 4 1 2 4 1 3 4   3 1 4 2 1 4 2   2 4 1 2 4 1 3 4   3 1 4 2 1 4 2 **etc.**

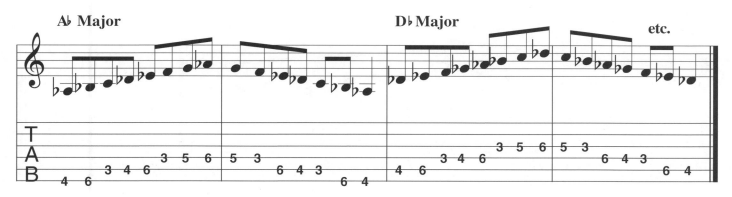

LESSON THREE

12 Bar Blues Riff Number 2

In lesson one a 12 bar riff was introduced. It involved the use of a basic shape, starting on the A, D or E note, matching the respective chords of the 12 bar chord progression.
The 12 bar Blues riff style can also involve more than one basic riff. In the example below, riff number 2 is used throughout the progression, except for the last bar. This last bar makes use of a very common ending for Blues riffs.

 6

Riff Two

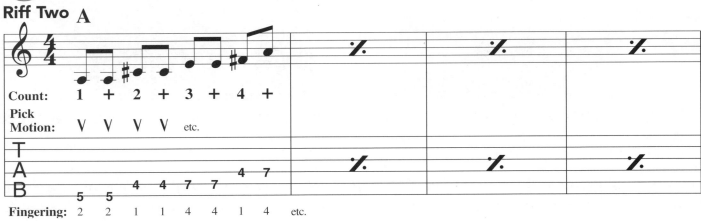

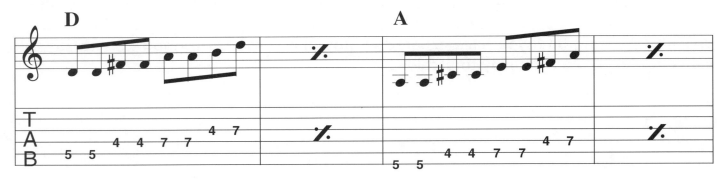

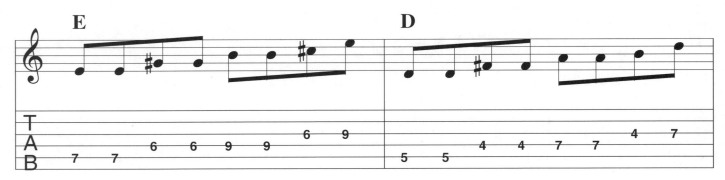

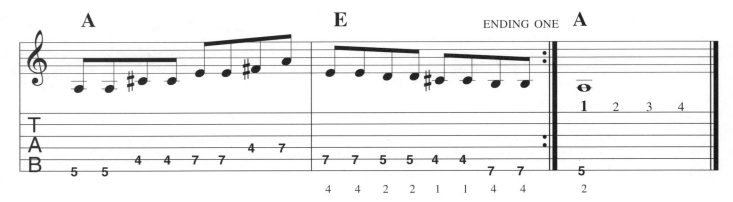

12 Bar Blues Riff Number 3

Riff number 3 is played over 2 bars and is used for the first eight bars of the progression. In bars 9 and 10 riff no.1 is used (a one bar riff) and in bars 11 a new ending is introduced.

7

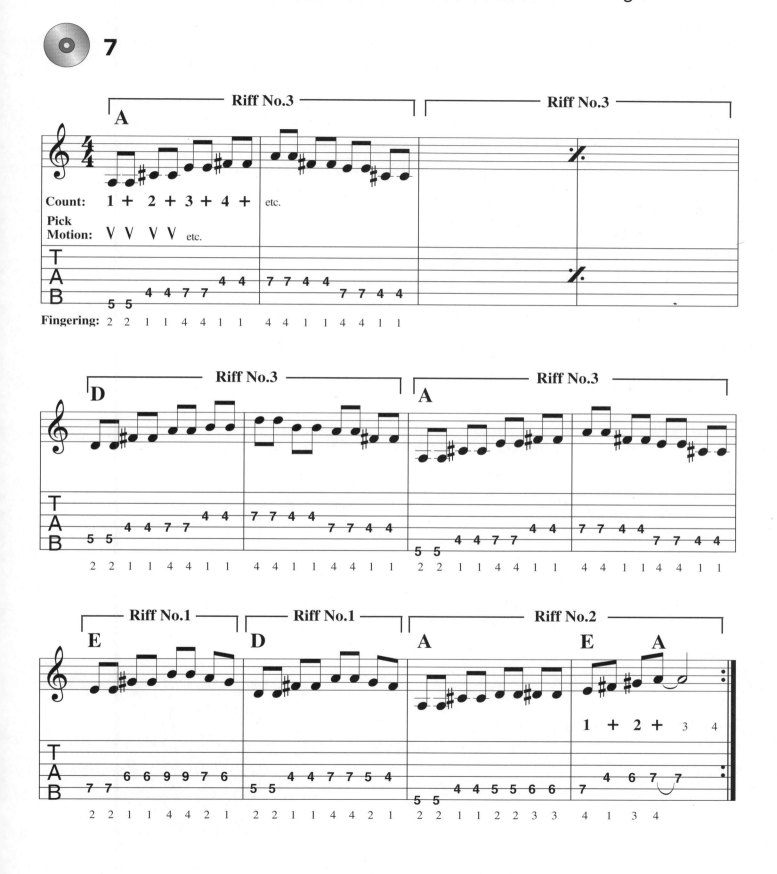

LESSON FOUR

Alternate Picking

All previous exercises have involved playing the notes with a downward motion of the pick, which is represented thus: **V**. In the exercise below, the technique of using down and up (**∧**) picking is introduced. This is called alternate picking, and it is essential for the development of speed and accuracy.

8.0 Begin on the 6th string and continue on the 5th, 4th, 3rd, 2nd and 1st strings and then play back down to the 6th string.

8.1

The pattern of notes that you are playing in this exercise will look like this on a fretboard diagram:

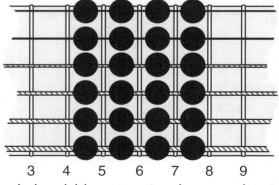

This is purely an exercise to loosen up your fingers and should be practiced every day in all positions on the fretboard, (e.g. starting at the first fret and working through to the 12th fret etc.).

12 Bar Blues Riff Number 4

The following one bar riff uses alternate picking. In this example downstrokes occur 'on' the beat and upstrokes occur 'off' the beat.

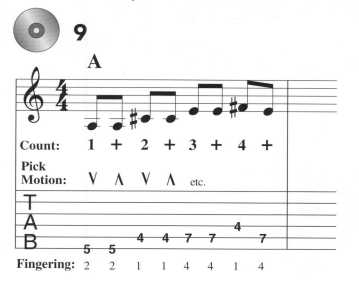

Repeat this riff shape throughout the 12 bar Blues progression, as outlined in earlier lessons.

Here are two more riffs using alternate picking. Once again, apply these riffs to the whole 12 bar progression.

10 (12 bar riff no.5)

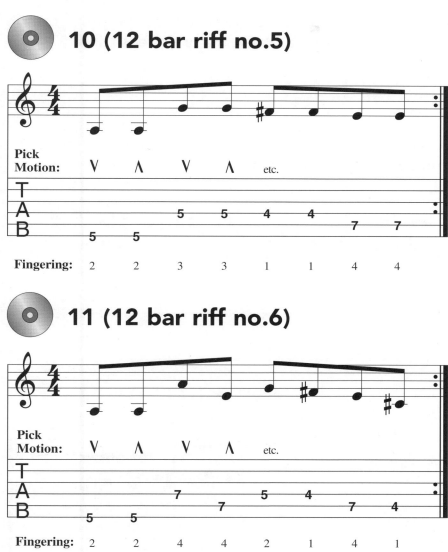

11 (12 bar riff no.6)

You should now practice the riffs given in earlier lessons using this alternate picking technique. All future lessons will involve alternate picking.

LESSON FIVE

The Major Scale - 2 Octaves

In lesson two you were introduced to a one octave pattern of the major scale. This pattern can be extended to cover two octaves, as illustrated in exercise 12.

 12

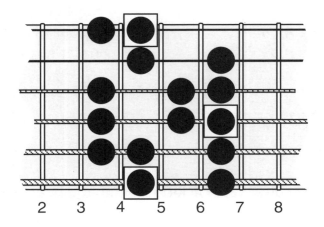

2 3 4 5 6 7 8

This pattern can commence on any note of the 6th string which will be the root note of the scale. Use alternate picking. In the exercise above, the A major scale is used.

13

Here is an exercise to help you become more familiar with the two octave major scale. Take it slowly at first and use alternate picking throughout.

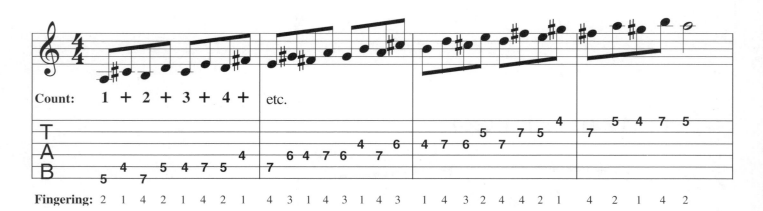

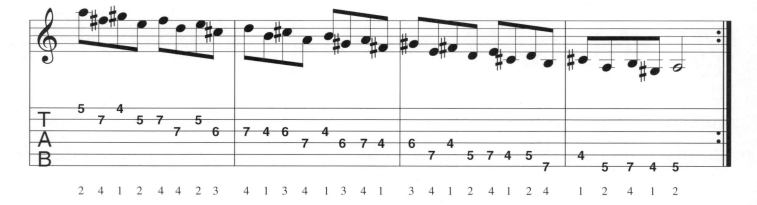

12 Bar Blues Riff Number 7

Riff number 7 involves the use of **lead-in notes**, which are notes that are played before the first full bar of music.

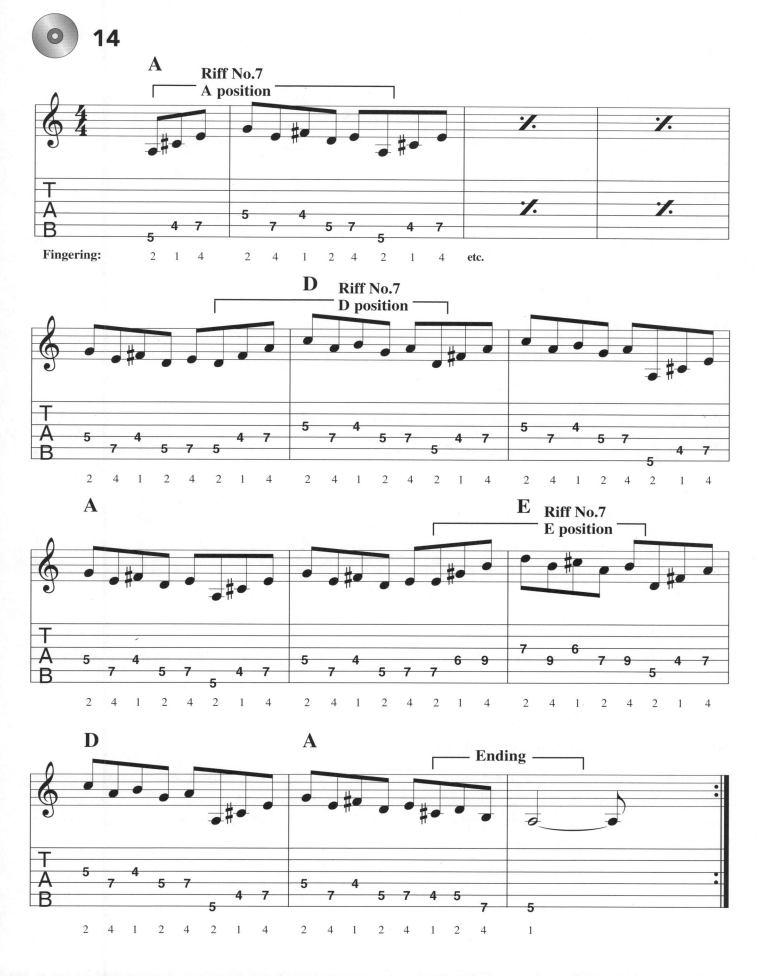

Riff Number 8

Riffs can be played against virtually any chord progression (i.e. not just 12 bar Blues). The following example illustrates a one bar riff played against the Am, Gm and Fm chords.

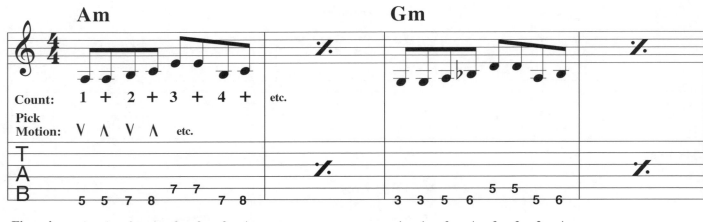

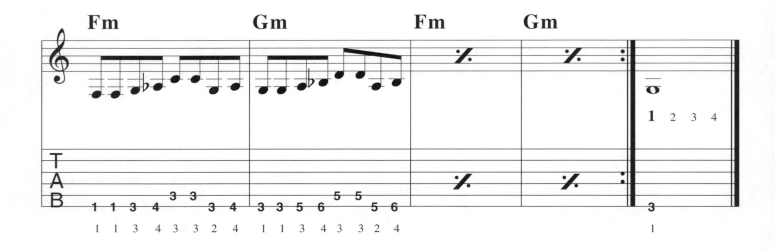

To maintain a smooth sound in this riff, use the fingering as indicated and use alternate picking.

SECTION ONE SUMMARY

This first section has involved some important preliminary exercises for lead guitar playing. You have been introduced to basic guitar riffs and scales, with the aim of developing dexterity and left/right hand co-ordination. You should now revise each lesson thoroughly before proceeding.

SECTION 2
Improvisation

Improvisation can be defined as being the spontaneous creation of a melody line. That is, when given a rhythm background (i.e. a chord progression) the improvisor is playing a lead melody to blend with it. The improvised lead is spontaneous in that it is not pre-learned (rather, it is done 'on the spot'), and it is unlikely to ever be repeated in exactly the same way.

Although improvising involves spontaneity and originality, there are certain scales, techniques and 'licks' that all Rock guitarists use. These important fundamentals will be discussed in the following lessons.

LESSON SIX

The Blues Scale

The Blues scale consists of $\underline{I}$ $\flat\underline{III}$ * $\underline{IV}$ $\underline{V}$ $\flat\underline{VII}$ ** notes of the major scale. Thus the A Blues scale is derived:

A major scale:

A	B	C#	D	E	F#	G#	A
$\underline{I}$	$\underline{II}$	$\underline{III}$	$\underline{IV}$	$\underline{V}$	$\underline{VI}$	$\underline{VII}$	$\underline{VIII}$

A Blues scale:

A	C	D	E	G	A
$\underline{I}$	$\flat\underline{III}$	$\underline{IV}$	$\underline{V}$	$\flat\underline{VII}$	$\underline{VIII}$

These notes can be arranged into patterns for simplification of learning and playing. The most common of these patterns is called pattern 1, and is outlined below:

16 (Pattern one Key of A)

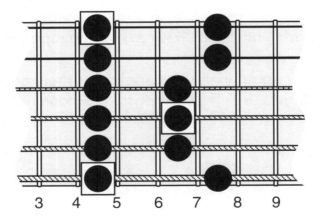

3 4 5 6 7 8 9

This pattern is used by every Rock lead guitarist and you should memorize it and practice it every day.

Pattern one can be used for improvising against the Blues progression in the key of A. Record yourself playing a 12 bar in A, using any rhythm you like. Now play through pattern one (playing one note per beat) and observe how the notes blend in with the 12 bar chords. Notice that any note from pattern one can be played against any chord in the progression.

This Blues pattern can be used to improvise against any Blues pattern in the key of A. 'Jamming' progressions have been included on the accompanying compact disc for you to practice improvising (see pages 92 to 97). The Blues scale can also include the flattened 5th note ($\flat\underline{V}$). This is discussed in more detail on page 54.

---

* $\flat\underline{III}$ indicates that the 3rd note of the scale is flattened.

** $\flat\underline{VII}$ indicates that the 7th note of the scale is flattened.

Triplets

Now that you know what notes to play, you have to learn how to play them. This will involve learning, amongst other things, various techniques that all lead guitarists use. One of the most common of these techniques is the use of **triplets**, which can be defined as three evenly spaced notes played in one beat (indicated thus ⌐3¬ *). They should be played with an accent on the first of each three (i.e. accent each note that falls on the beat, creating a 'waltz' feel.

BLUES SCALE - TRIPLETS

(To be played against the 12 bar Blues progression). Each note of pattern one can be numbered as such:

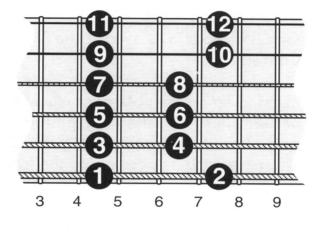

17

Triplets can be played in the following order.

⌐3¬	⌐3¬	⌐3¬	⌐3¬	
>	>	>	>	
1 2 3	2 3 4	3 4 5	4 5 6	etc.

Pick Motion: V ∧ V   V ∧ V   V ∧ V   V ∧ V

Count: **1 + a**   **2 + a**   **3 + a**   **4 + a**   etc.

Be sure to follow the correct pick motion (alternate picking) and count 1+a,2+a,3+a,4+a, accenting the first note of each three (indicated by the arrowhead >).

Also play the major scale using triplets.

To conclude this lesson, try some improvising by playing various note combinations of pattern one against your recording of the 12 bar Blues in A. Play slowly and carefully at first, since accuracy is more important than speed at this stage.

*In music, these are referred to as eighth note triplets.

LESSON SEVEN

Transposing

The term 'transposing' is used to describe the process whereby a progression (or song) is changed from one key to another. So far you have only been introduced to pattern one in the key of A. To transpose this pattern to other keys it can be related to the root 6 bar chord, which has the same name as the key of the Blues, e.g.

Blues in A: The root 6 A major bar chord is located at the 5th fret, so pattern one will be played at the 5th fret (as in lesson six).

Blues in E: The root 6 E major bar chord is located at the 12th fret, so pattern one will be played at the 12th fret.

Blues in G: The root 6 G major bar chord is located at the 3rd fret, so pattern one will be played at the 3rd fret.

Play pattern one in different keys as far up the neck as practicable. You will notice that once you pass the 12th fret, the pattern starts repeating E.g. pattern one played at the first fret will be the F Blues scale. Pattern one played at the 13th fret will also be the F Blues scale. The table below sets out pattern one and its position on the fretboard for every key.

KEY	PATTERN 1 FRET LOCATION
E	Open and 12th
F	1st and 13th
F♯/G♭	2nd and 14th
G	3rd and 15th
A♭	4th and 16th
A	5th and 17th
B♭	6th and 18th
B	7th and 19th
C	8th
D♭/C♯	9th
D	10th
E♭	11th

Hence pattern one in the key of A can now be played in two different positions.

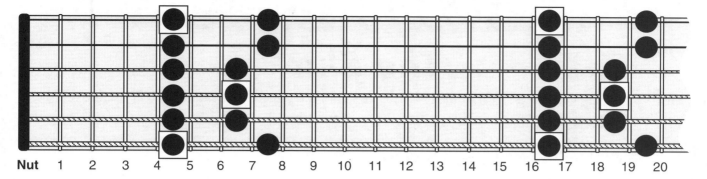

Each note in pattern one at the 17th fret is one octave higher than the corresponding note in pattern one at the 5th fret. Practice moving between these two patterns to add variety in your improvising. Also practice playing in different keys and become thoroughly familiar with the relative position of each octave pattern. The following 12 bar Blues uses pattern 1 in the keys of A (5th and 17th fret), D (10th fret) and E (12th fret). Notice the use of minor chords in this progression. 12 bar Blues can use many different types of chords including major, minor and seventh chords.

18

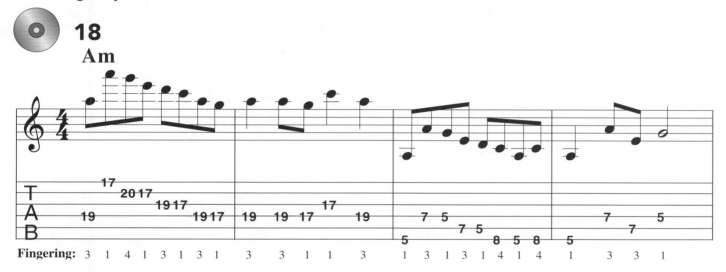

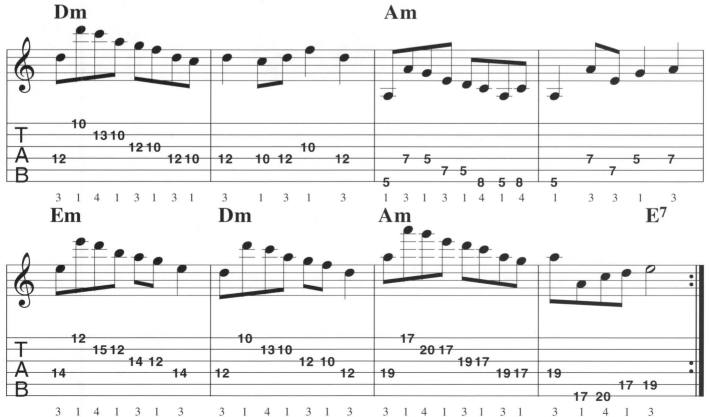

LESSON EIGHT

The Slur

The slur is one of the most popular techniques used by lead guitarists. It is indicated by a curved line joining the notes in question, as such:

19.0 The Hammer-on
(ascending slur)

The Hammer-on is performed by playing the first of the two notes, and then while it is still sounding, the left hand finger hammers down onto the 2nd note (see photos above). Thus the second note (D) is not picked; the sound is produced entirely by the left hand finger 'hammering-on' to the string. A hammer-on is indicated by the letter **H**.

19.1 The Pull-off
(descending slur)

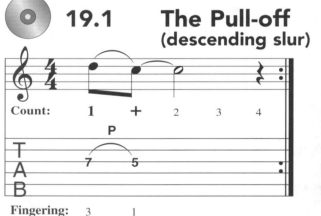
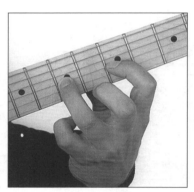

The Pull-off is performed with both fingers in position before the first note is played (see photos). This is necessary because when the first note (D) has been played, the finger flicks the string as it lifts off; creating the sound of the lower note (C). The following example makes use of both hammer-ons and pull-offs. A pull-off is indicated by the letter **P**.

20

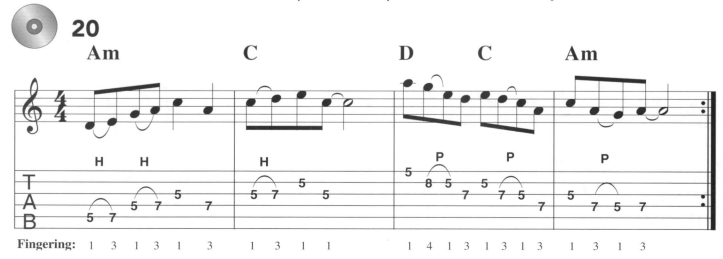

Hammer-ons and pull-offs may be played together, as in the following exercise. This exercise is continuous and only the first note in each bar is played with the pick. It involves rapid slurring and can be used for any two notes from pattern one which are on the same string.

21

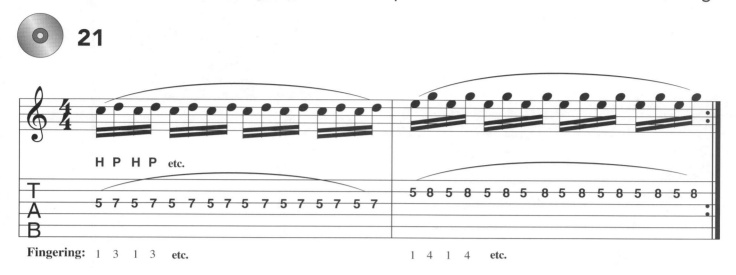

The previous exercises can be referred to as Rock 'licks'. Rock licks can be defined as small musical phrases that are frequently used by lead guitarists. They involve the use of techniques such as the slur, discussed above. It is most important for you to learn as many licks as possible and listen for their use in lead solos (see Appendix 4 on ear training). In the following lessons, many common licks will be shown.

COMBINING TECHNIQUES

Techniques can be combined to create interesting Rock licks. The following exercises use triplets in conjunction with slurs.

22

For exercise 23.0 the first finger bars across the 2nd, 3rd and 4th strings.

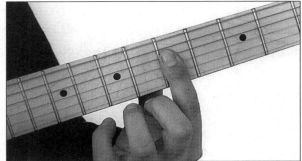

23.0

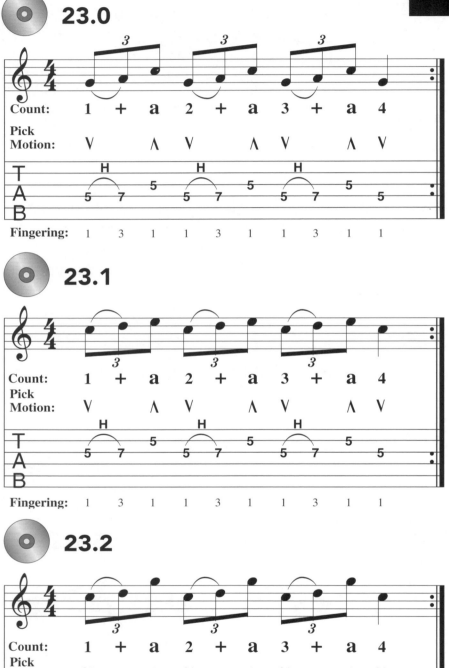

23.3 Play the 3 previous exercises in the following order:

EX 23.0   **EX 23.1**   **EX 23.2**   **EX 23.1**

The following exercise consists of several licks joined together to form a solo. This solo is played over a minor chord progression. Using pattern one in minor keys is discussed in detail in lesson 12.

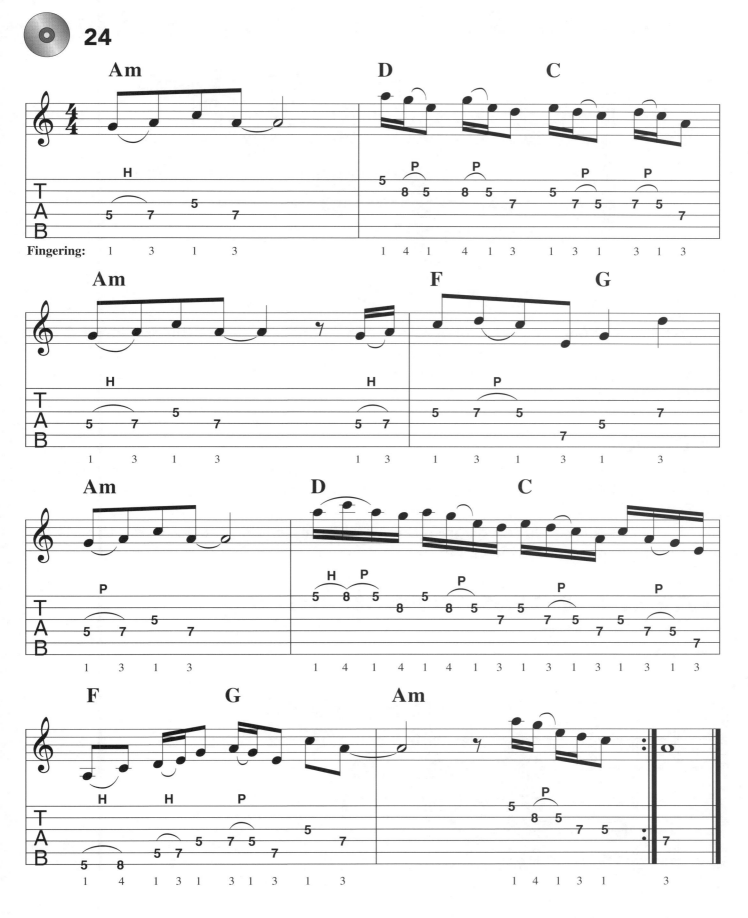

LESSON NINE

Pattern One Extension (Key of A)

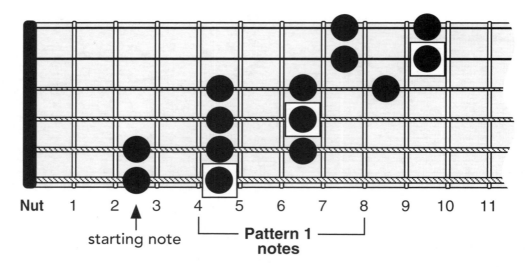

This extension of pattern one involves 5 additional notes, located at the 3rd, 9th and 10th frets. Be sure to play this pattern correctly, starting with the G note on the 6th string at the 3rd fret. Remember that this Blues pattern is still in the key of A (e.g. improvise against a Blues in A.

THE SLIDE

The slide is a technique which involves a finger moving along the string to its new note. The finger maintains pressure on the string, so that a continuous sound is produced.

Slides occur as marked in the diagram below. When ascending the scale, the third finger is used for sliding; when descending, the first finger is used.

PATTERN 1 - EXTENSION FINGERING

25

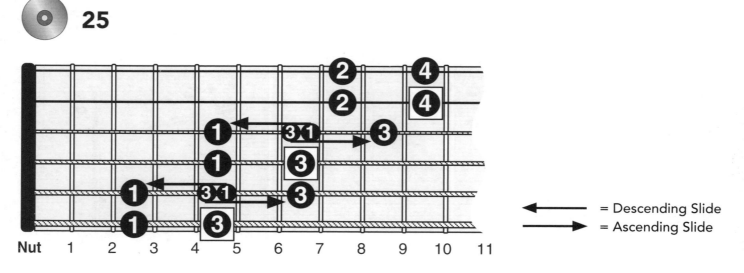

When sliding, make sure that your finger remains in contact with the string.

In music and tablature, the slide is indicated by a straight line joining the two notes in question, accompanied by the letter **S**.

26

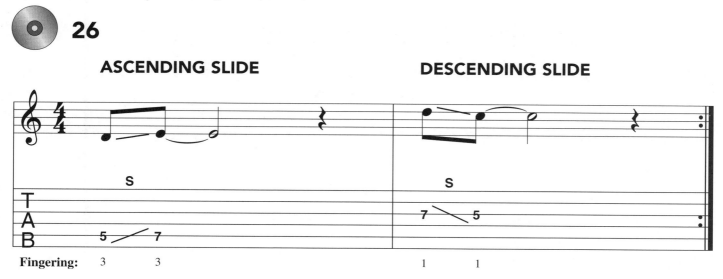

The slide technique can be used between any two notes on the same string, and you should experiment with different combinations. The following exercises demonstrate how slides can be used in creating licks.

27

28

The first slide in the following example is a "quick" slide. Select a lower note and slide to the note in the tab quickly without giving any time value to the first note. A quick slide is indicated by a line and number only. The first note is not notated in the tablature.

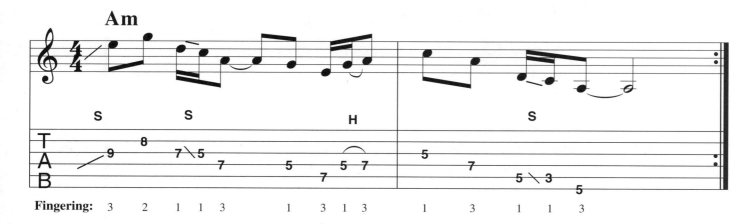

LESSON TEN

Major Key Progressions

So far most of your improvising has been based on Blues Progressions. This involved using the Blues scale, which contains the notes $\underline{\text{I}}$, $\flat\underline{\text{III}}$, $\underline{\text{IV}}$, $\underline{\text{V}}$, $\flat\underline{\text{VII}}$, relative to the major scale.

When a progression is in a major key, but does not have a 'Blues sound' (e.g. most melodic 'pop' songs) a different scale is used for improvising. This scale is called a **major pentatonic*** scale and contains the notes $\underline{\text{I}}$, $\underline{\text{II}}$, $\underline{\text{III}}$, $\underline{\text{V}}$, $\underline{\text{VI}}$, relative to the major scale.

An example of a major key progression is the **turnaround**:

TURNAROUND IN A

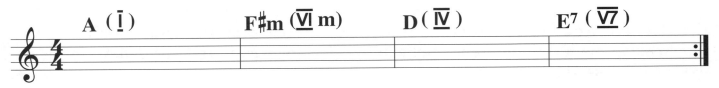

A ($\underline{\text{I}}$)   F#m ($\underline{\text{VI}}$ m)   D ($\underline{\text{IV}}$)   E^7 ($\underline{\text{V7}}$)

Finish the progression with a single strum on the 1st chord (A major).

For improvising against this progression, the A major pentatonic scale is used. It contains the notes:

A	**B**	**C#**	**E**	**F#**
$\underline{\text{I}}$	$\underline{\text{II}}$	$\underline{\text{III}}$	$\underline{\text{V}}$	$\underline{\text{VI}}$

These notes can be arranged into the following pattern.

PATTERN 1 - MAJOR KEY PROGRESSIONS

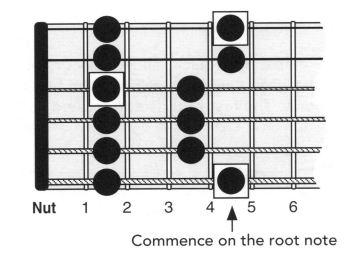

29

Nut   1   2   3   4   5   6

Commence on the root note

You will notice that this pattern is identical in shape to pattern one for Blues progressions, but it contains different notes and is played three frets lower.

*Pentatonic meaning 5 tones

30

Here is a lick which uses this pattern against the A major key progression shown on the previous page. Notice the use of quick slides, explained on page 33.

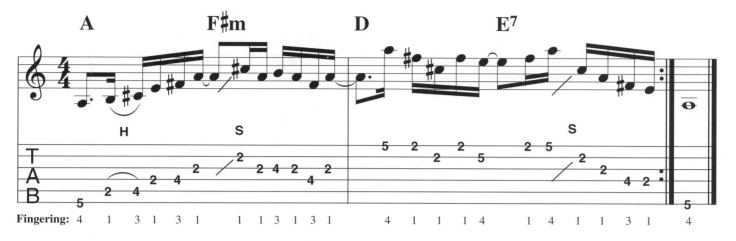

Here is a comparison of the two scales which use pattern one:

A Blues scale: Pat. one - 5th fret   **A   C   D   E   G   A**

A Major pentatonic scale: Pat. one - 2nd fret   **A   B   C♯   E   F♯   A**

This major pentatonic pattern can be used to improvise against any major key progression in the key of A. 'Jamming' progressions have been included on the accompanying CD (see page 94) for you to practice with. Once you are familiar with the new application of pattern one, use its extension as introduced in lesson nine. The table below sets out the relationship between the location of pattern one for Blues and Major key progressions.

KEY	BLUES PROGRESSION	MAJOR KEY PROGRESSION
A	5(17)	2(14)
B♭	6(18)	3(15)
B	7(19)	4(16)
C	8	5(17)
D♭/C♯	9	6(18)
D	10	7(19)
E♭	11	8
E	12	9
F	1(13)	10
F♯/G♭	2(14)	11
G	3(15)	12
A♭	4(16)	1(13)

You may notice from this table that for major key progressions pattern one is following the root 6 relative minor bar chord. (for more information on relative minor keys, see Appendix 1).

LESSON ELEVEN

The Bend

The bend is a technique which involves pushing a string upwards (or downward), which will raise the pitch of the fretted note being played. The most common bend is that of a tone (2 frets), however, bends of one fret or three frets (or more) are sometimes used. An example of a two fret bend, from D to E, can be written in two ways:

 **31.0**

QUICK BEND (on the beat - count "one")

Fingering: 3

31.1

SLOW BEND (count "one and")

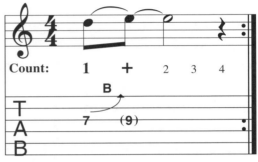

Fingering: 3

In this photograph 3 fingers are used to push the string upwards. The number of fingers used in a bend will depend upon the convenience and/or the position of the note you wish to bend.

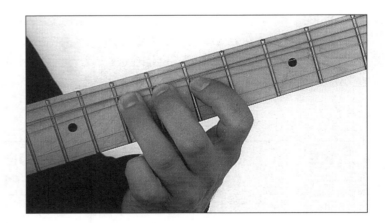

THE REVERSE BEND

A reverse bend is played from the bent note, returning to the original note.

 31.2

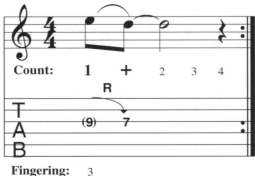

Fingering: 3

* As it is difficult at first to bend to the correct pitch, you should use very light gauge strings on your electric guitar to begin with. Later you may wish to experiment with heavier strings, as they produce a stronger tone.

When improvising, you should bend only to a note that is in the scale. This is very difficult, so you should first listen to the note you are going to bend to (to establish its pitch) and then attempt the bend, e.g. in the D to E bend example just given, play the E note first to establish its pitch and then attempt the bend.

 **32**

This Rock lick uses a quick bend from D to E, followed by a slow reverse bend back to D.

 **33.0**   In this exercise, each bend is held while the following note is played.

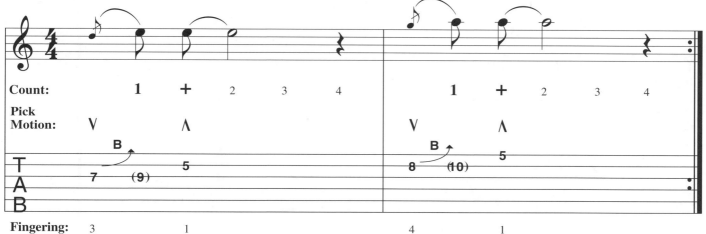

 **33.1**

In this example, the note E on the second string is played at the same time as the bend on the third string.

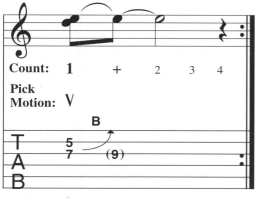

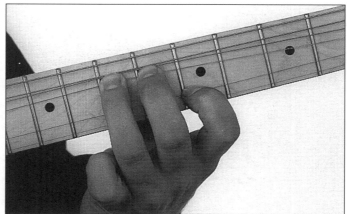

Exercise 33.2 is a combination of the previous two exercises. For ease of playing, the first finger bars across the first and second strings as shown in the photo below.

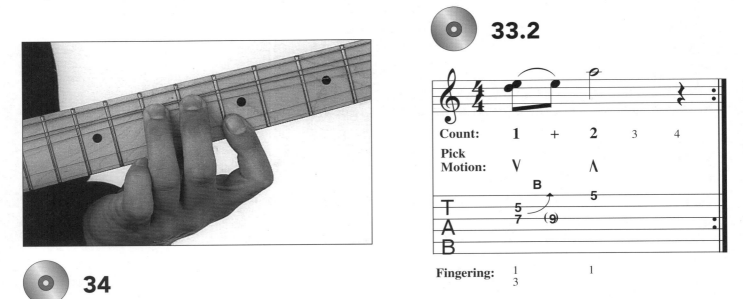

Here is a solo which uses all of the types of bends you have learnt in this lesson.

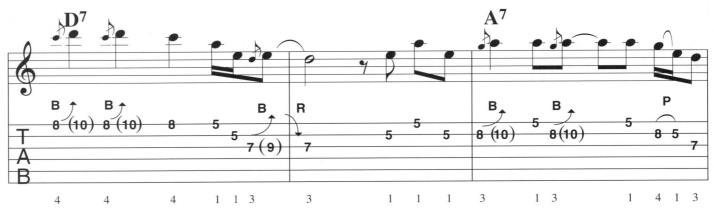

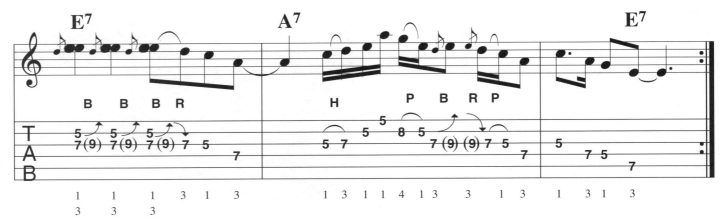

LESSON TWELVE

Minor Key Progressions

In lesson 10 you were introduced to improvising against a progression (song) in a major key using pattern one (as a major pentatonic scale). Many songs, however, are written in a **minor key**, an example of which is given below.

(Finish on an Am chord)

This progression is in the key of A minor, starting and ending on an Am chord.

For improvising against a minor key, pattern one is located on the same fret as the root 6 minor bar chord which has the same name as the key. E.g. for the key of A minor, the root 6 Am bar chord is located at the 5th fret, and so pattern one is played in this position.

The scale you are playing when improvising against minor key progressions is referred to as a **minor pentatonic** scale.

 35

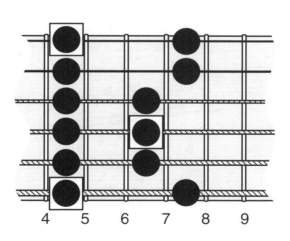

You will notice that pattern one for the key of A minor is located in the same position as pattern one for a Blues progression in the key of A major.*

Record the minor progression above, and improvise using pattern one and its extension. Remember to make use of all the Rock licks and techniques studied so far.

This minor pentatonic pattern can be used to improvise against any minor key progression in the key of A minor. On pages 95 and 96 you will find examples of minor key 'jamming' progressions which are included on the accompanying CD.

*This is because the Blues Rock sound is based on the use of minor scale notes against a major key progression.

PICK TREMOLO

The pick tremolo involves rapid pick movement on a given note, hitting the string as many times as possible within a certain period. This period will be preset in written music and a tremoloed note is notated as such:

36

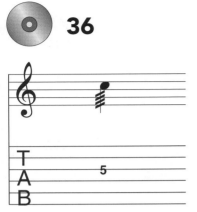

Fingering: 1

The diagonal lines indicate a tremolo, and in this example as many C notes as possible are played in one count. Hold the pick close to the tip as illustrated in the above photo and keep it rigid, rapidly moving your hand from the wrist. Do not move your forearm. Play through pattern one, tremoloing each note. When improvising, the duration of a tremoloed note is up to your own discretion.

37

The following example uses pick tremolo on two notes played together and is played over a chord progression in the key of A minor.

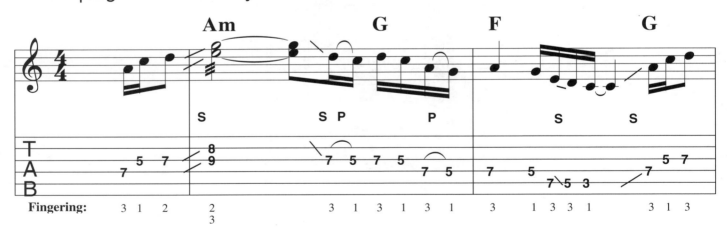

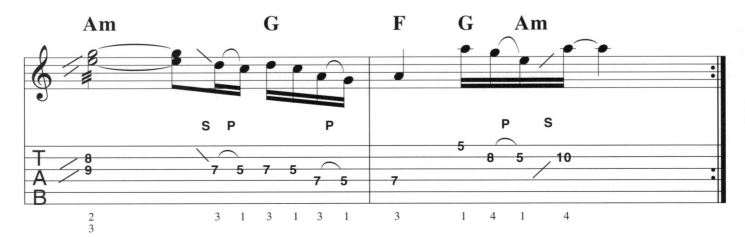

LESSON THIRTEEN

The Major Pentatonic Scale in Blues Improvising

In Blues progressions, the major pentatonic scale can also be used for improvising (e.g. use pattern one at the 2nd fret for a Blues in A). This will result in a more melodic style of lead playing. Try playing against the Blues progressions on pages 92 and 93 using the major pentatonic scale.

It is also possible to use the Blues and major pentatonic scales for improvising within the same progression. In this situation you can change back and forth from one scale to the other. Many of the great Blues and Rock players (e.g. BB King, Eric Clapton, Jimi Hendrix, Stevie Ray Vaughan) create melodies from a combination of these scales. This concept is taken even further in Jazz, where many different scales may be combined when improvising, even over one chord. Combining scales can be confusing at first, so make sure you have control of the notes of each scale individually before attempting to combine them. In the example below, both the major pentatonic and Blues scales are used to create a Chuck Berry style lead.

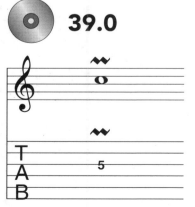

38

THE VIBRATO

One of the most difficult techniques used by lead guitarists is the vibrato. This involves pushing the strings up and down (like a rapid series of short bends) which adds slight pitch variations to the basic note

39.0

The vibrato is used to make a note sound more interesting and sustain that note. You should practice the vibrato with each of the four left hand fingers. The vibrato is indicated by a wavy line as such: ∿

THE VIBRATO/BEND COMBINATION

The vibrato can be applied to a note which has been bent to its new pitch, e.g:

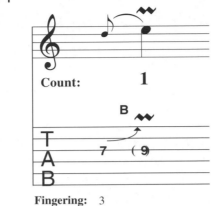

39.1

Here is a lead guitar solo which makes use of vibrato and vibrato combined with bending. It uses pattern one and pattern one extension in the key of A minor and incorporates all of the techniques you have learnt.

40

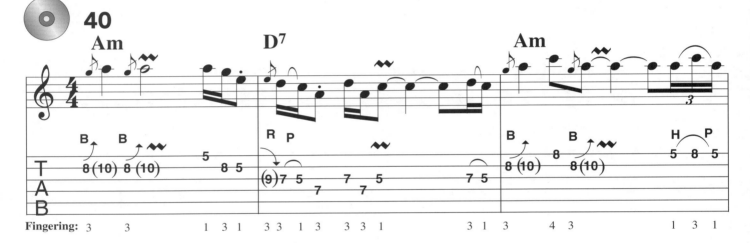

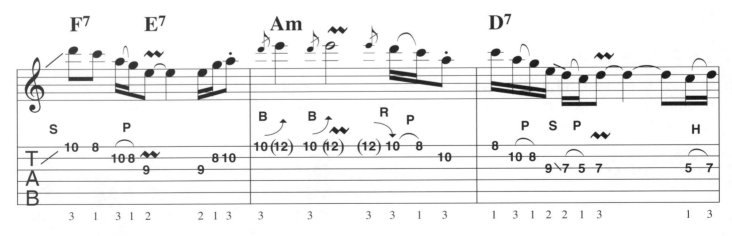

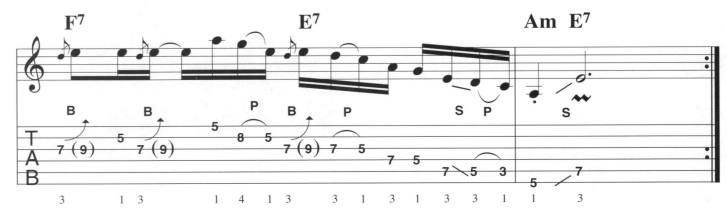

LESSON FOURTEEN

Summary of Pattern One

In this section so far you have learnt pattern one (and its extension) and applied it in three different ways, i.e. improvising with Blues progressions, major key progressions and minor key progressions in any key. The table below sets out the relationship between the location of pattern one for each of these different progressions:

KEY	BLUES PROGRESSIONS (Blues Scale)	MAJOR KEY PROGRESSIONS (Major Pentatonic)	MINOR PROGRESSIONS (Minor Pentatonic)
A	5th fret	2nd and 14th frets	5th fret
B♭	6th	3rd and 15th	6th
B	7th	4th and 16th	7th
C	8th	5th	8th
D♭/C#	9th	6th	9th
D	10th	7th	10th
E♭	11th	8th	11th
E	12th	9th	12th
F	1st and 13th	10th	1st and 13th
F#/G♭	2nd and 14th	11th	2nd and 14th
G	3rd and 15th	12th	3rd and 15th
A♭	4th and 16th	1st and 13th	4th and 16th

Pattern one can be related to a root 6 bar chord in each of the three different progressions.

BLUES Progressions: Pattern one occurs at the same position as the root 6 major bar chord having the same name as the key.

MAJOR KEY Progressions: Pattern one occurs at the same position as the root 6 relative minor bar chord (3 frets lower).

MINOR KEY Progressions: Pattern one occurs at the same position as the root 6 minor bar chord having the same name as the key.

You should now practice improvising in any key, playing any of the three types of progressions listed.*

In the next 3 lessons you will learn to extend each of the 3 scales so far discussed (i.e. Blues, major and minor pentatonic) over the entire fretboard, by the introduction of more patterns.

*A list of Blues, major and minor key progressions can be found on pages 92 to 97.

LESSON FIFTEEN

PATTERN FOUR

Altogether there are five basic fingering patterns which cover the entire fretboard in any key when placed end to end. After pattern one, the next most common improvising pattern is pattern four. It has a similar but not identical shape to pattern one and is illustrated below.

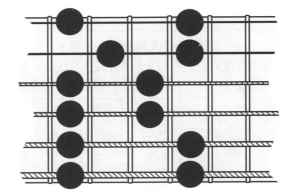

Memorize this pattern and practice it in all positions. You will notice that no root note has been given. Its root note is determined by which of the three types of progressions it is applied to.

PATTERN FOUR - BLUES (Key of A)

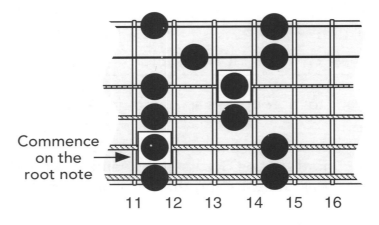

Commence
on the
root note →

11   12   13   14   15   16

Pattern four, for Blues progressions, occurs in the same position as the root 5 major bar chord having the same name as the key, e.g. Blues in A - the root 5 A bar chord is located at the 12th fret, and so pattern four is played in this position. If you analyze the notes in pattern four, you will see that you are still playing the notes of the A Blues scale (A, C, D, E, G).

PATTERN FOUR - MINOR KEY PROGRESSIONS (Key of A minor)

Pattern four, for minor key progressions, occur at the same position as the root 5 minor bar chord having the same name as the key, e.g. Progression in A minor - the root 5 Am bar chord is located at the 12th Fret, so pattern four will be played at this position. This is the same position as for a Blues progression in the key of A as shown in the above diagram.

The following lick uses pattern 4 at the 12th fret. It is played here against an A minor chord. As you can hear, this is a very bluesy lick and would work equally well against any chord from a Blues progression in the key of A.

41

Fingering: 1   4   1   3   1   3   2   3   3   4   3   1   3

PATTERN FOUR - MAJOR KEY PROGRESSIONS (Key of A)

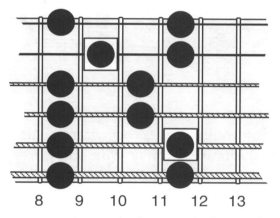

      8   9   10   11   12   13

Pattern four, for major key progressions, is located three frets lower than the same pattern for Blues, i.e. it occurs at the same position as the root 5 relative minor bar chord, e.g. major chord progression in A - the relative minor chord is F#m, located as a root 5 bar chord at the 9th fret, and so pattern four is located in this position. Once again, you are playing the same notes (A, B, C#, E, F#) as in pattern one for major key progressions.

The following lick makes use of pattern 4 at the 9th fret against a chord progression in A major. Now that you know how to use pattern four for each of the three types of progressions, practice playing it in all keys.

42

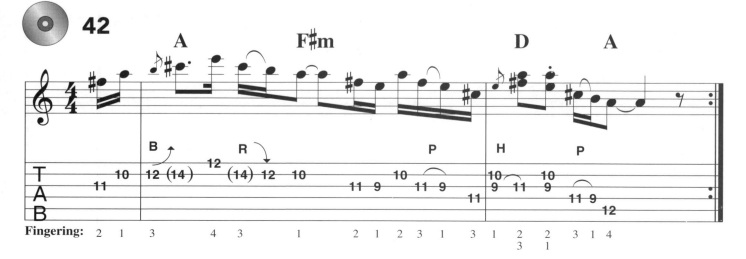

Fingering: 2   1   3   4   3   1   2   1   2   3   1   3   1   2   2   3   1   4
                                                                          3   1

LESSON SIXTEEN

Patterns One and Four Combination

When pattern one (and its extension) and pattern four are combined, the overall pattern on the fretboard can be represented thus:

A MAJOR BLUES SCALE/A MINOR PENTATONIC SCALE

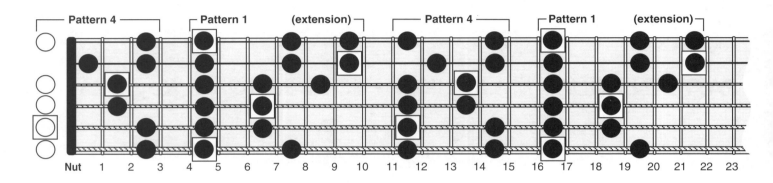

Practice and memorize this pattern combination in the key of A for Blues, major key and minor key progressions. For major key progressions, the entire pattern moves 'down' three frets to the left. Once you are familiar with the pattern in the key of A, transpose it to other keys, e.g. E, G, etc.

 43

The following lick uses both pattern 1 extension and pattern 4. Notice how using different patterns makes it possible to play the same notes in more than one place on the fretboard.

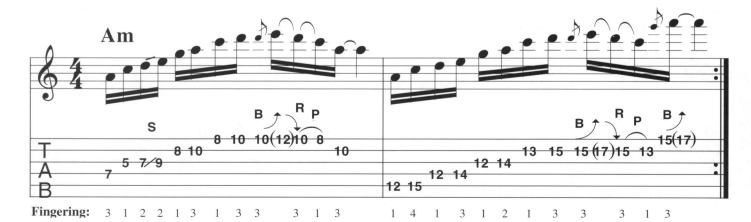

PATTERN FIVE

By combining patterns one and four you create another pattern which links them together - pattern five.

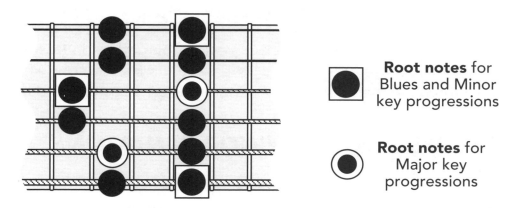

Root notes for Blues and Minor key progressions

Root notes for Major key progressions

For a Blues in A, pattern five starts at the 3rd and 15th frets. For a major key progression in A, pattern five starts at the 12th fret. For a minor key progression in A minor, pattern five starts at the 3rd and 15th fret.

These next two licks demonstrate the use of pattern 5. The first one is played over an A minor chord and uses pattern 5 at the 3rd fret. The second one is played over a progression in A major and uses pattern 5 at the 12th fret.

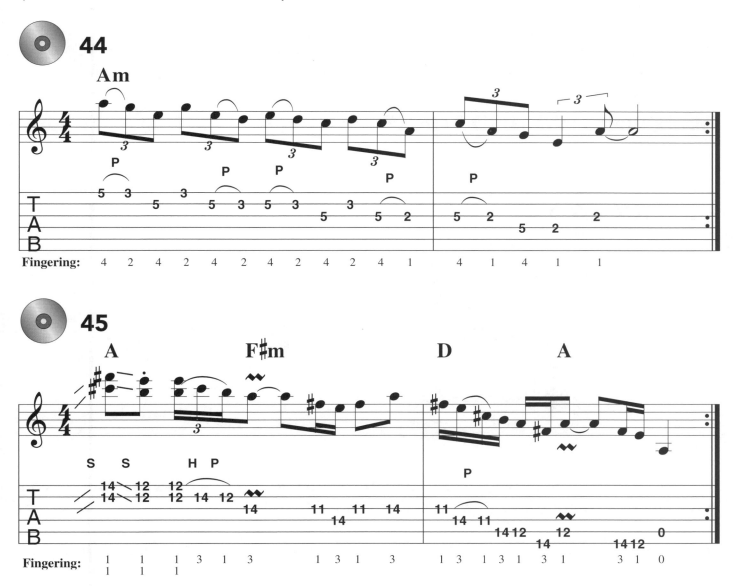

LESSON SEVENTEEN

The Complete Pattern

By adding only three more notes (and their octaves) to the pattern in lesson 16, the entire fretboard is now covered (these added notes have been marked by crosses so that you will instantly recognize them). Remember that this entire pattern uses only 5 different notes.

A MAJOR BLUES SCALE/A MINOR PENTATONIC SCALE

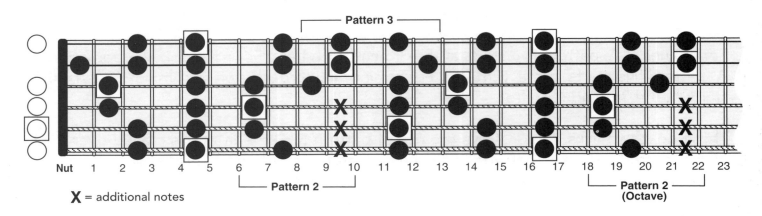

X = additional notes

Memorize this complete pattern by continual practice and application to different keys. Remember that for major key progressions the entire pattern moves 'down' 3 frets to the left.

PATTERNS TWO AND THREE

The extra notes added create two new patterns, as illustrated below.

PATTERN TWO

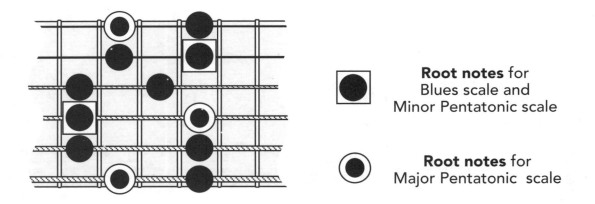

Root notes for Blues scale and Minor Pentatonic scale

Root notes for Major Pentatonic scale

For a Blues in A, pattern two starts at the 8th and 20th frets. For a major key progression in the key of A, pattern two starts at the 5th and 17th frets.

For a minor key progression in A minor, pattern two starts at the 8th and 20th frets.

46

Here is a lick derived from pattern two at the 8th fret.

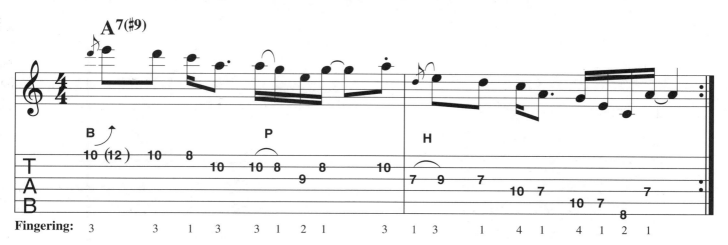

PATTERN THREE

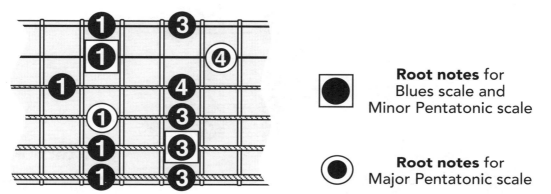

Root notes for
Blues scale and
Minor Pentatonic scale

Root notes for
Major Pentatonic scale

This pattern covers a span of five frets and the fingering to be used is written on the dots which represent the notes.

For a Blues in A, pattern three starts at the 10th fret. For a major key progression in the key of A, pattern three starts at the 7th and 19th frets. For a minor key progression in A minor, pattern three starts at the 10th fret.

 47

The following lick uses pattern three at the 10th fret.

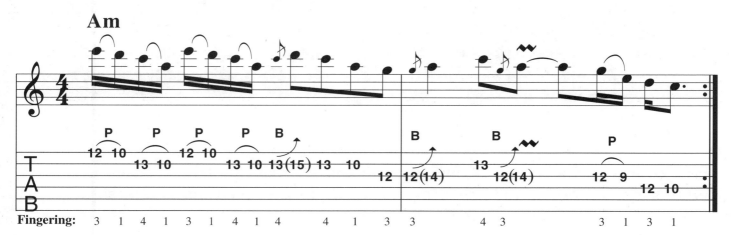

LESSON EIGHTEEN

Summary of Patterns

Outlined below are the five patterns studied in this section.

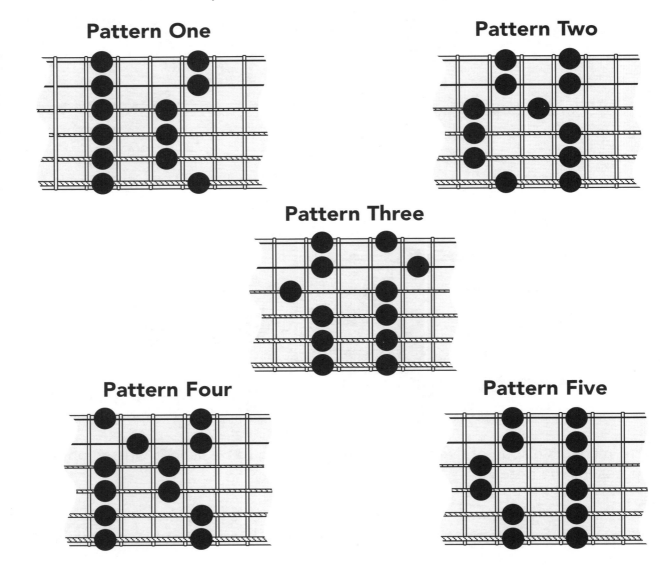

Pattern One

Pattern Two

Pattern Three

Pattern Four

Pattern Five

A combination of these patterns covers the entire fingerboard as such:

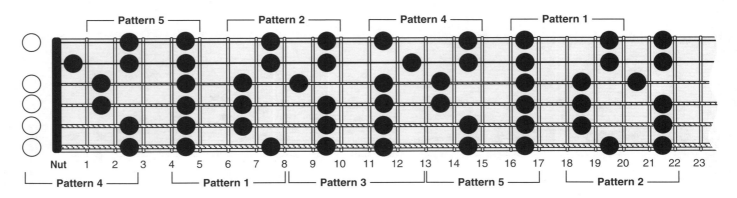

This example is the A Blues/A minor pentatonic/C major pentatonic scale. Use these patterns in their respective keys to improvise against the 'jamming' progressions (pages 92 to 97) which are on the accompanying CD.

48

The following lead guitar solo moves between all of the five patterns. Notice how the notes work equally well against all of the chords. This is because the chords belong to the keys of both C major and A minor which are relative keys and as mentioned on the previous page, the patterns you have learnt can be described as A minor pentatonic or C major pentatonic.

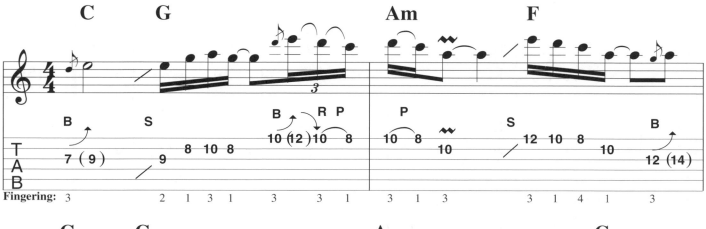

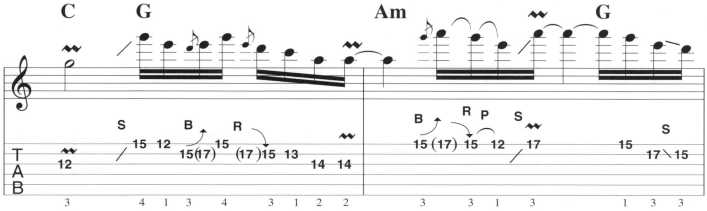

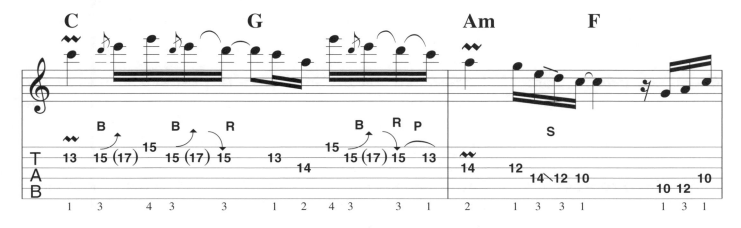

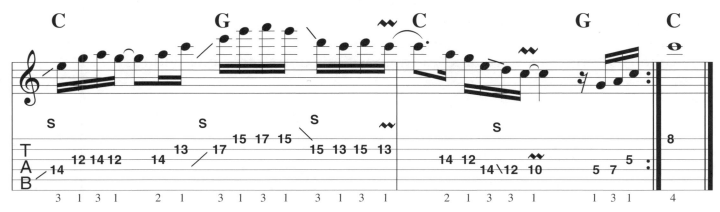

The table below illustrates the starting fret position for each of the five patterns in all keys.

KEY	PATTERN 1		PATTERN 2		PATTERN 3		PATTERN 4		PATTERN 5	
	Blues and Minor Keys	Major Key	Blues and Minor Keys	Major Key	Blues and Minor Keys	Major Key	Blues and Minor Keys	Major Key	Blues and Minor Keys	Major Key
A	5(17)	2(14)	8	5(17)	10	7	12	9	3(15)	12
Bb	6	3(15)	9	6	11	8	1(13)	10	4(16)	1(13)
B	7	4(16)	10	7	12	9	2(14)	11	5(17)	2(14)
C	8	5(17)	11	8	1(13)	10	3(15)	12	6	3(15)
Db/C#	9	6	12	9	2(14)	11	4(16)	1(13)	7	4(16)
D	10	7	1(13)	10	3(15)	12	5(17)	2(14)	8	5(17)
Eb	11	8	2(14)	11	4(16)	1(13)	6	3(15)	9	6
E	12	9	3(15)	12	5(17)	2(14)	7	4(16)	10	7
F	1(13)	10	4(16)	1(13)	6	3(15)	8	5(17)	11	8
F#/Gb	2(14)	11	5(11)	2(14)	7	4(16)	9	6	12	9
G	3(15)	12	6	3(15)	8	5(17)	10	7	1(13)	10
Ab	4(16)	1(13)	7	4(16)	9	6	11	8	2(14)	11

Remember that patterns one and four can be related to bar chords for each of the three different types of progressions, i.e.

Blues Progressions: Pattern one occurs in the same position as the root 6 major bar chord having the same name as the key, and pattern four the root 5 major bar chord having the same name as the key.

Major Key Progressions: Pattern one occurs in the same position as the root 6 relative minor bar chord of the key, and pattern four occurs in the same position as the root 5 relative minor bar chord of the key.

Minor Key Progressions: Pattern one occurs in the same position as the root 6 minor bar chord having the same name as the key, and pattern four the root 5 minor bar chord having the same name as the key.

The other patterns can be related to the positions of patterns one and four.

SECTION 3

In the previous section you were introduced to the basic scales for improvising against Blues, major key and minor key progressions. These basic scales can be expanded upon by the use of additional notes, passing notes and harmony notes.

LESSON NINETEEN

Additional Notes - Blues Scale

An additional note is a note which does not belong to the scale, but can be used against most chords in a progression without sounding out of key. The notes of the Blues scale are $\bar{I}$, $\flat\bar{III}$, $\bar{IV}$, $\bar{V}$, $\flat\bar{VII}$ (revise lesson 6) and so for an A Blues scale the notes A, C, D, E and G are used. One additional note is the $\flat\bar{V}$, which for the key of A is an E♭ note.

PATTERN ONE - BLUES SCALE - KEY OF A

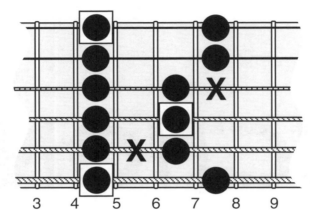

Experiment using this new note in your improvising. Draw a fretboard diagram (21 frets), adding the E♭ ($\flat\bar{V}$) note to the A Blues scale, and become familiar with its position in each pattern. The following lick uses the Blues scale with the extra E♭ note and moves through patterns one, two and three.

49

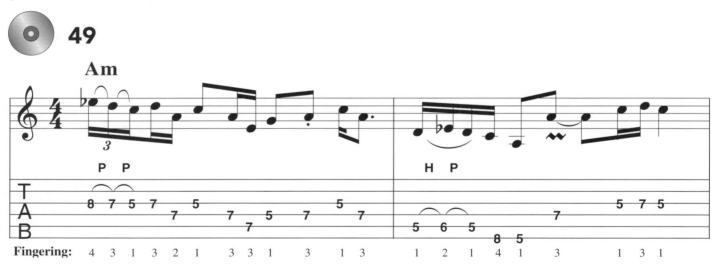

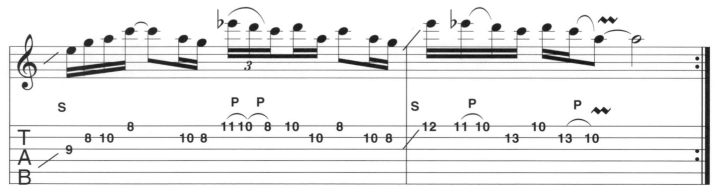

Other notes which may be added to the Blues scale are $\overline{\text{II}}$, $\overline{\text{III}}$, and $\overline{\text{VI}}$ notes of the major scale. In the key of A these additional notes are B, C♯ and F♯.

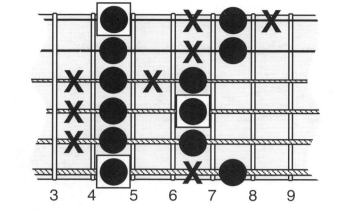

As before, draw up a fretboard diagram and add these extra notes to the Blues scale. Remember that additional notes will not always blend in with all the chords of a Blues progression, whereas the Blues scale notes will. Here is a short solo which makes use of these extra notes.

50

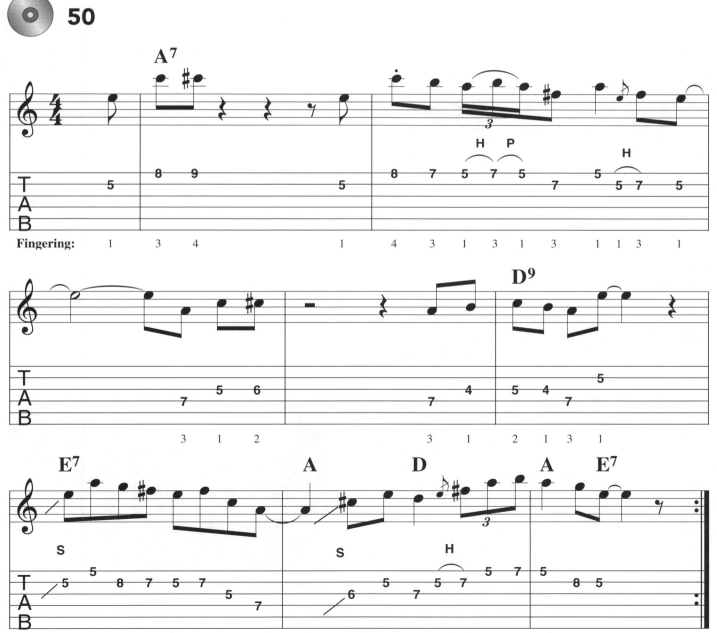

ROCK LICKS

The following Rock licks involve the use of additional notes to the Blues, played with a triplet rhythm.

51.0   Pick only the first note (all the others are slurred).

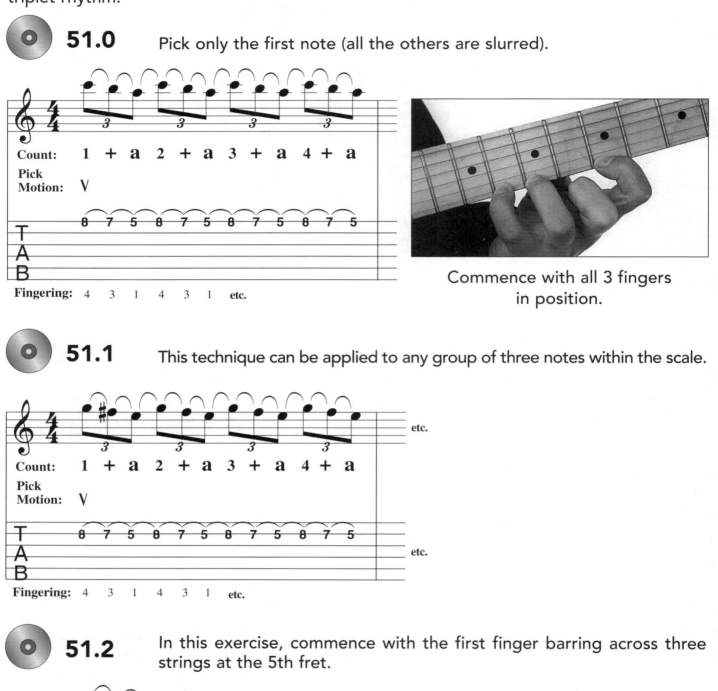

Commence with all 3 fingers
in position.

51.1   This technique can be applied to any group of three notes within the scale.

51.2   In this exercise, commence with the first finger barring across three strings at the 5th fret.

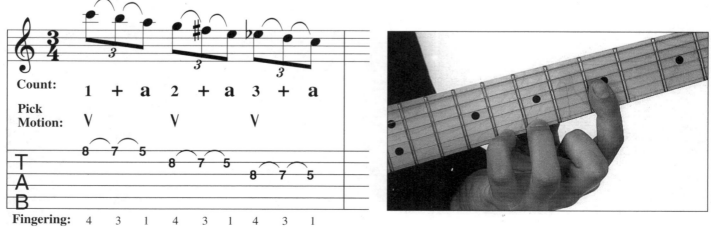

You should apply the licks studied in this lesson to other scale patterns.

LESSON TWENTY

Major Pentatonic Scale - Additional Notes

The major pentatonic scale contains the $\overline{\mathrm{I}}$, $\overline{\mathrm{II}}$, $\overline{\mathrm{III}}$, $\overline{\mathrm{V}}$, and $\overline{\mathrm{VI}}$ notes of the major scale. As additional notes, the $\overline{\mathrm{IV}}$ and $\overline{\mathrm{VII}}$ can be added, to complete the major scale. Thus, for improvising against a major key progression, the major scale can be used, with emphasis on the major pentatonic notes.

PATTERN ONE - KEY OF A

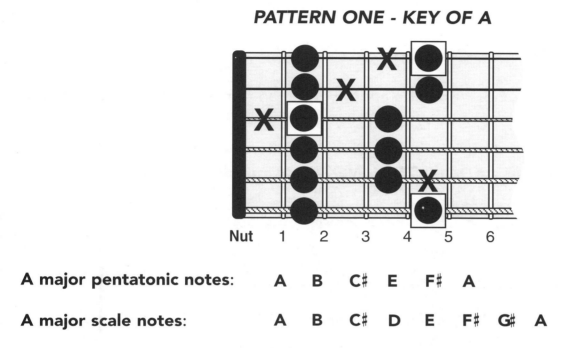

A major pentatonic notes:	A	B	C♯		E	F♯		A
A major scale notes:	A	B	C♯	D	E	F♯	G♯	A

To produce the major scale sound (DO RE MI FA SO LA TI DO), start on the root note (as marked with a square around the dots).

Here is the complete fretboard diagram for the A major pentatonic scale with additional notes (ie. the A major scale).

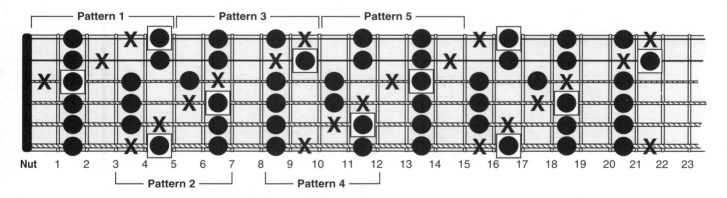

Notice that pattern two is the same major scale pattern that you were introduced to as an exercise in lesson 5.

As well as for improvising, the major scale is most useful for playing the melodies of songs in major keys. (For a detailed study of how to use the major scale, see *Progressive Scales and Modes for Guitar*).

LESSON TWENTY ONE

Minor Pentatonic Scale - Additional Notes

The minor pentatonic scale contains the notes $\bar{I}$, $\flat\bar{III}$, $\bar{IV}$, $\bar{V}$, $\flat\bar{VII}$ of the major scale. For example:

A Major Scale :	A	B	C#	D	E	F#	G#	A

A Minor Pentatonic Scale :	A		C	D	E		G	A

As additional notes, the $\bar{II}$ and $\flat\bar{VI}$ can be added, giving an A minor 'pure' scale* with the notes:

	A	B	C	D	E	F	G	A

PATTERN ONE - ADDITIONAL NOTES (A minor 'Pure' Scale)

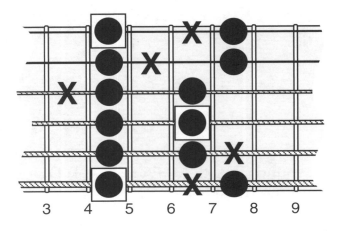

This minor scale contains the same notes as the C major scale, except that it starts and finishes on A (A is the root note).

To create a very distinctive 'minor sound', the 7th note (in this case G#) can also be added. This will give the following notes in pattern one.

PATTERN ONE - KEY OF A

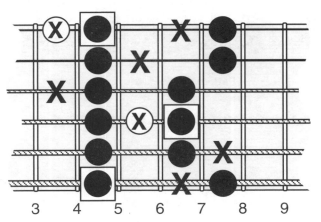

*See Appendix 1 for a more detailed explanation of minor scales.

Here is the entire fretboard with the A minor pentatonic scales and additional notes. Remember to transpose them to other keys.

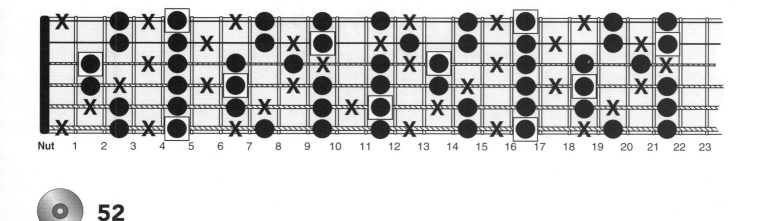

52

Here is a 2 bar riff in the key of A minor, using the additional note G♯. In the first bar, two notes are played together by barring the second and third strings with the first finger.

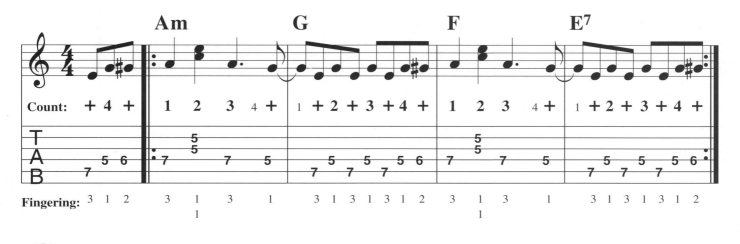

53

The following lick makes use of all of the extra notes which can be added to the minor scale pattern, with the 7th note (G♯) replacing the ♭7 (G). When this combination of notes is used, the **harmonic minor scale** is created. For more information on different types of minor scales, see *Progressive Scales and Modes for Guitar*.

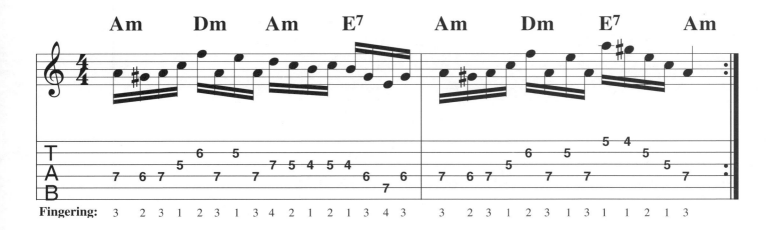

LESSON TWENTY TWO

Open String Slurs

In lesson 19 you were introduced to Rock licks using triplets and continuous slurs. This technique can also involve the use of an open string, as such:

 54

In this exercise, only the first note is picked. No other note is picked throughout the entire exercise.

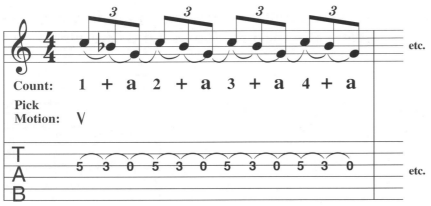

 55

Here is another example of an open string slur:

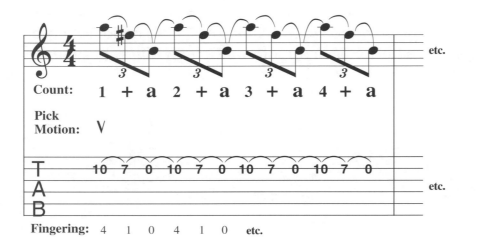

For the A note, you can use either your third or fourth finger.

RIGHT HAND FRETTING TECHNIQUE

A technique that is used in conjunction with open string slurring is the fretting of the string with the right hand. The photograph below illustrates how this is done.

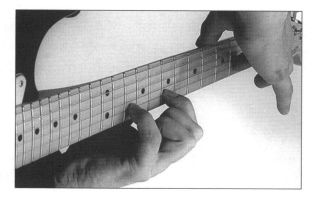

In this photo the right hand is pressing behind the third fret.

 56   In this exercise the first note is played by hammering on with the fourth finger.

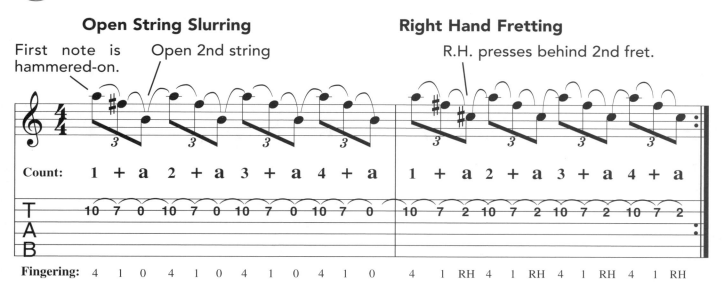

Open String Slurring

First note is hammered-on.

Open 2nd string

Right Hand Fretting

R.H. presses behind 2nd fret.

The right hand can fret any note between the nut and the left hand, so you should experiment with other combinations.

RIGHT HAND BENDING TECHNIQUE

Another technique that can be used with any type of slurring is the bending of the string with the right hand, behind the nut. The photograph below illustrates this (notice the position of the right hand).

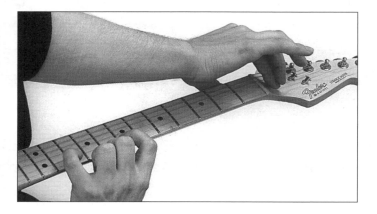

Right hand finger presses string down.

LESSON TWENTY THREE

Harmony Notes

Harmony notes are the simultaneous combination of two or more sounds. The most common harmonies used in lead playing are thirds and sixths. Octaves are also used (although these are not technically harmony notes).

THIRDS

Thirds are any two notes that have an interval of a third between them. This interval can be calculated by counting up three notes from the lower note, including the lower note as the first of the three, e.g.:

C to **E** is a third: **C**   **D**   **E**
D to **F** is a third: **D**   **E**   **F**

Here is the C scale in thirds:

57

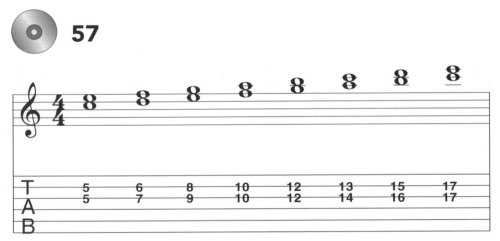

This gives a pattern on the fretboard as such:

THIRDS: 2ND AND 3RD STRING PATTERN

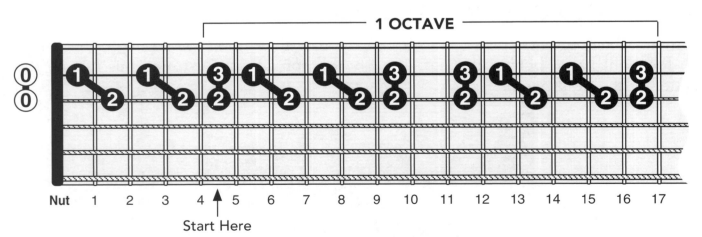

Play this pattern up and down against either a C major or A minor chord progression, and memorize it. You can either use a pick, or the second and third fingers, as shown in the following photo.

For the key of C major, start at the 5th fret as marked. Thus you are starting on the fret at which pattern one is located. Practice playing this pattern of thirds in other keys, e.g. for the key of G, the pattern starts at the 12th fret (or in the open position) as does pattern one (you will find it more convenient to play down from the 12th fret, rather than continue up the fretboard).

Thirds can also be played on the 1st and 2nd strings, giving the following pattern:

THIRDS: 1ST AND 2ND STRING PATTERN

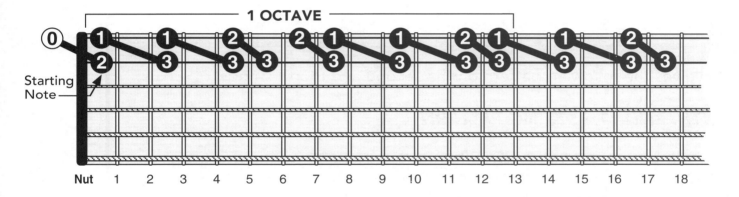

The above pattern can also be played on the 6th and 5th strings, the 5th and 4th strings and the 4th and 3rd strings. In each case, firstly locate the root note for the key you are in. This root note will be on the lower (in pitch) of the two strings. E.g. here is the C scale in 3rds, on the 4th and 5th strings.

58

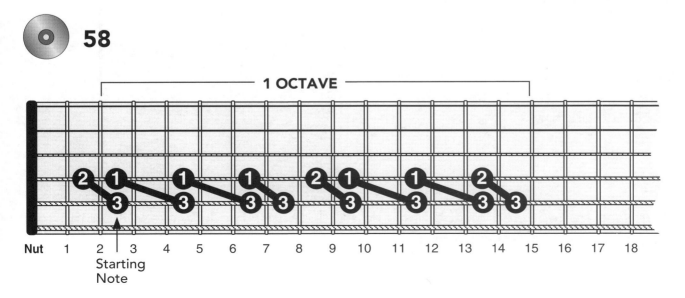

LESSON TWENTY FOUR

SIXTHS

The interval of a sixth can be calculated by counting up six notes from the lower note, e.g:

C to **A** is a 6th: **C D E F G A**

G to **E** is a 6th: **G A B C D E**

In scales of 6ths, the harmony notes are most commonly played a 6th below the scale note..

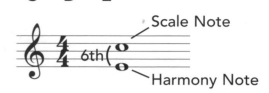

Here is the C scale in 6ths.

59

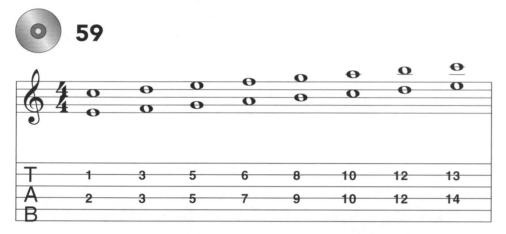

This gives the following pattern on the second and fourth strings.

SIXTH: 2ND-4TH STRING PATTERN

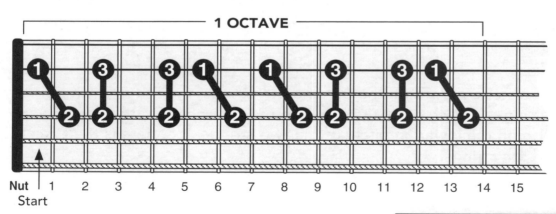

Use the pick to play the lower note and the third finger* to play the higher note, as illustrated in the photo.

This pattern can be repeated on the first and third strings. The keynote will be the top note (in pitch) of the two starting notes.

*By using the 3rd finger, the 2nd finger is left free to play other notes if desired.

60

Sixths played on the 4th and 6th strings, and the 3rd and 5th strings will involve a different pattern, as such:

SIXTH: 4TH-6TH, 3RD-5TH STRING PATTERN

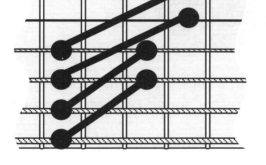

OCTAVES

Octave notes on the guitar can be played with the following string combinations:

3rd-1st strings
4th-2nd strings
5th-3rd strings
6th-4th strings

 61

Here is the pattern for the C scale, using the 5th and 3rd strings.

C SCALE OCTAVES: 5TH-3RD STRING PATTERN

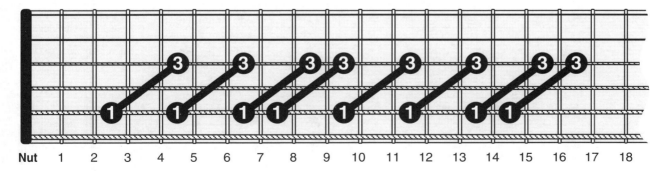

The use of harmony notes is only touched on briefly here. For a more in-depth study of how to use 3rds, 6ths and octaves, see *Progressive Funk and R&B Guitar Technique*, *Progressive Blues Guitar Licks* and *Progressive Blues Guitar Solos*.

Octaves can be played by using the pick for the lower note, and the third finger for the higher note.

Octaves can also be played with the pick, by 'deadening' the middle string between the two fretted notes with the first finger. Thus all 3 strings are strums without the middle string being sounded.

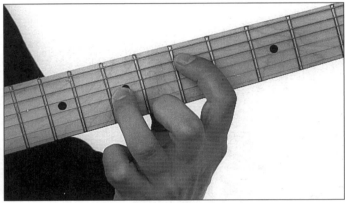

 62

The first half of this exercise is played using the pick and the third finger and the second half is played with the pick only. Listen to the different sound produced by each of these techniques.

LESSON TWENTY FIVE

An Alternative Improvising Method

So far your improvising has been based on key centers, i.e. the key of a song is determined, and then improvising patterns within that key are played against any chord in the song. Thus in the following example, pattern one could be used at the 2nd* fret throughout (e.g. major key progression in A), without changing its position as the chords change. In this way the use of pattern one is in relation to the key (A) rather than each individual chord change.

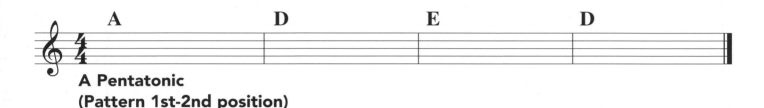

A Pentatonic
(Pattern 1st-2nd position)

Another approach to improvising is to treat each chord separately, i.e. changing the key of your lead for each chord, e.g:

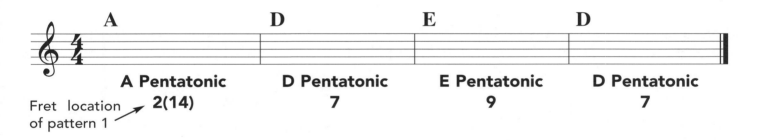

Fret location → of pattern 1

A Pentatonic	D Pentatonic	E Pentatonic	D Pentatonic
2(14)	**7**	**9**	**7**

Play this progression slowly, so that the position changes can be easily achieved.

Try other pattern combinations, but be sure to match the pentatonic scale name with the name of the chord, e.g:

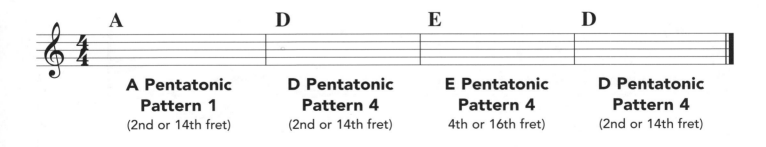

A Pentatonic	D Pentatonic	E Pentatonic	D Pentatonic
Pattern 1	Pattern 4	Pattern 4	Pattern 4
(2nd or 14th fret)	(2nd or 14th fret)	4th or 16th fret)	(2nd or 14th fret)

* This progression could also be treated as a Blues, with pattern one in the 5th position.

63

Here is an example which can be applied to this style of improvising.

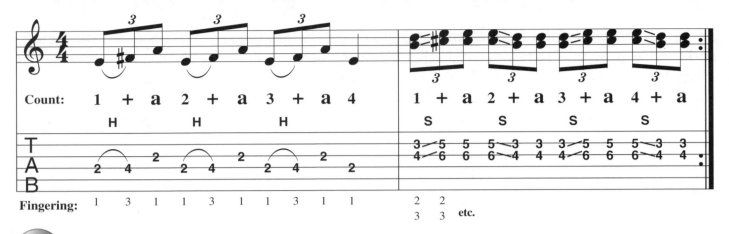

 64

Exercise 63 can be used against the chord progression on the previous page, playing 2 bars of each chord. For the A chord it is played at the 2nd fret, for the D chord it is played at the 7th fret and for the E chord it is played at the 9th fret.

65

This approach also works well for minor keys. The following exercise uses pattern one moved between the 5th, 10th and 12th frets to follow the chord changes.

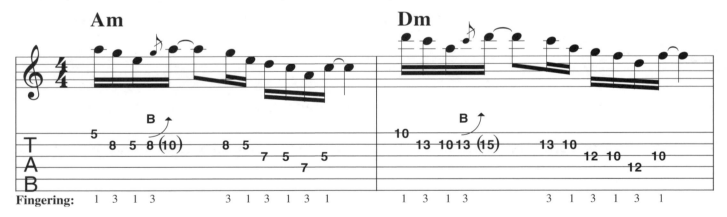

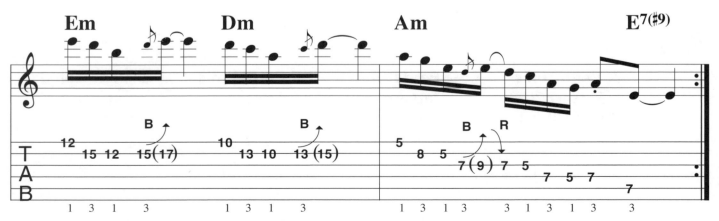

You should also experiment with other pattern combinations and other chord progressions (see pages 92 to 97).

LESSON TWENTY SIX

Playing With the Pick and Fingers

Lead guitarists sometimes use a technique of playing with both the pick and the fingers of the right hand. The right hand fingers are named as such:

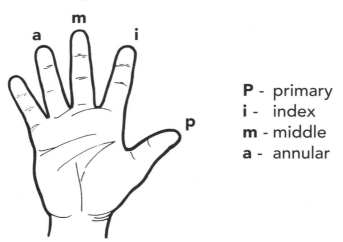

P - primary
i - index
m - middle
a - annular

BOOGIE RIFF

The following riff is often referred to as a 'boogie' and involves the use of the pick and the 'a' finger. The pick plays the bass notes, while the 'a' finger plays the A note on the third string.

66

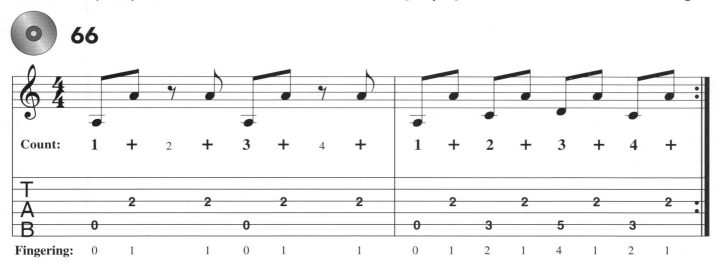

To create a rest on the '2' and '4' counts, the 4th finger lightly touches all strings, deadening the sound (illustrated in the photograph below).

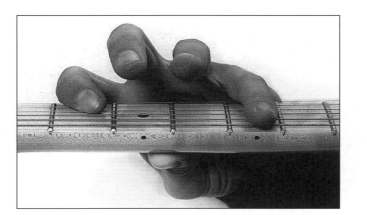

Here is a variation of the boogie, using the 'a' and 'm' fingers.

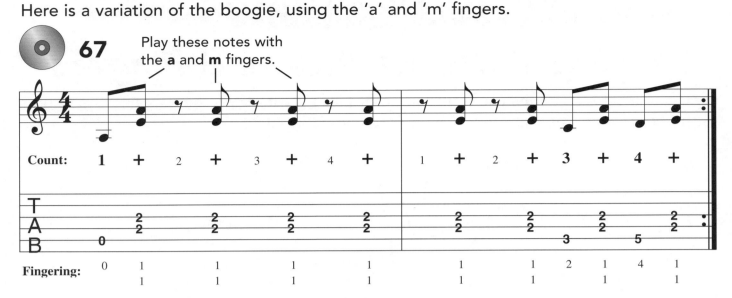

The following exercise combines the use of the pick with the 'm' and 'a' fingers. This exercise may be difficult at first, so play the first bar separately until the fingering becomes familiar.

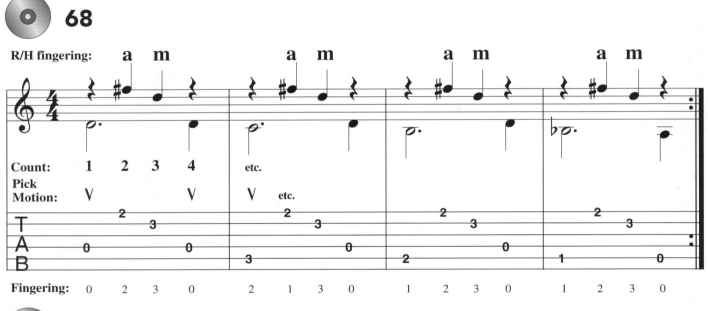

This lick is played with the pick and the 'm' finger in a similar manner to playing octaves. For more on playing with pick and fingers, see *Progressive Blues Guitar Licks* and *Progressive Blues Guitar Solos*.

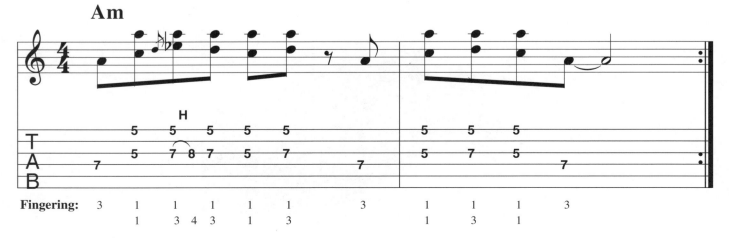

LESSON TWENTY SEVEN

Ideas For Further Study

This final lesson has been designed to provide you with some ideas for future study which are beyond the scope of detailed examination in this book. The pentatonic and major scales as applied so far are largely used by Rock, Blues, Country and commercial Pop guitarists. This incorporates a very wide range of music, however some styles, in particular Jazz and Jazz Rock, base their improvisation on different concepts.

CHORDAL IMPROVISATION

Chordal improvisation involves using the notes of each chord as the base for improvising. Consider the following progression:

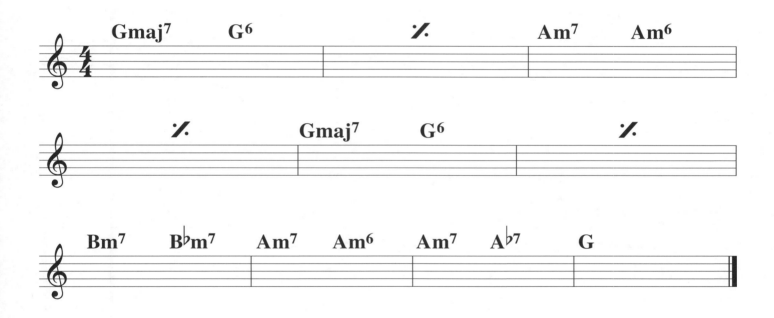

The key of this progression is G and you could improvise with the G pentatonic or major scales. However, a Jazz musician is more likely to use the chord notes as outlined below.

CHORD	CHORD NOTES			
Gmaj7:	G	B	D	F#
G6:	G	B	D	E
Am7:	A	C	E	G
Am6:	A	C	E	F#

CHORD	CHORD NOTES			
Bm7:	B	D	F#	A
B♭m7:	B♭	D♭	F	A♭
A♭7:	A♭	C	E♭	G♭
G:	G	B	D	

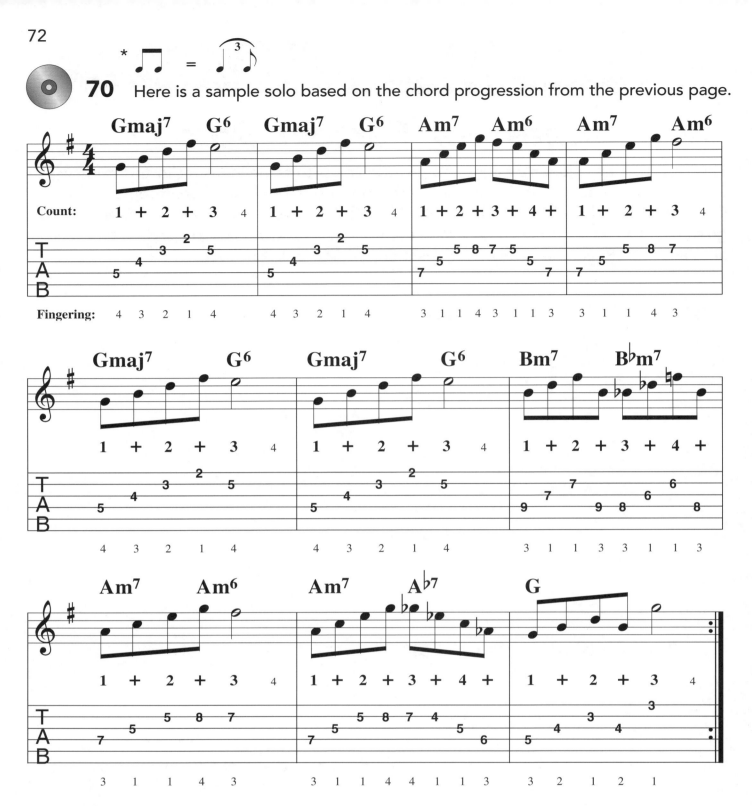

70 Here is a sample solo based on the chord progression from the previous page.

For chordal improvisation, the following areas of study are essential:

1. Chord construction – each chord type (e.g. major, minor, dominant 7th etc.) has a specific formula which relates to the major scale, e.g. the formula for a major chord is $\bar{1}$ - $\bar{3}$ - $\bar{5}$, which means that each major chord takes the first, third and fifth notes from its major scale – C major contains the notes C E G; A major contains the notes A C♯ E (see chord formula chart, page 81).

2. Notes in all positions – a complete knowledge of the guitar fretboard. This is best achieved by relating each position to two or three keys that are best suited to that position, and then playing through songs and exercises of graded difficulty.

3. Chord arpeggios – an arpeggio involves playing each individual note of a chord (rather than strumming it) and can be used as part of a lead solo.

*Notes written as eighth notes are to be played as the first and third notes of an eighth note triplet. This is referred to as 'swinging' the eighth notes.

Here is an example of chord arpeggios on the Gm, Gmaj7, G7 and G6 chords:

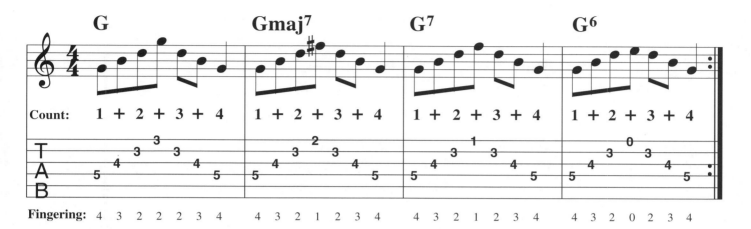

These studies must, of course be augmented by the playing and analysis of Jazz guitar solos.

MODAL IMPROVISING (Chord Scales)

A mode can be described as being a displaced scale. In other words, if you play a C major scale but starting and finishing on the D note, you are playing a mode:

D	E	F	G	A	B	C	D
$\underline{II}$	$\underline{III}$	$\underline{IV}$	$\underline{V}$	$\underline{VI}$	$\underline{VII}$	$\underline{I}$	$\underline{II}$

The roman numerals relate to the C scale.

This is called the **Dorian** mode and it is produced by playing through $\underline{II}$ - $\underline{II}$ on the major scale (e.g. D - D on the C scale). Each note of the major scale can be used as a tonic (starting note) for a different mode, and the situation can be summarized thus:

Roman numeral representation	Example using C scale								Mode name
$\underline{I}$ - $\underline{I}$	C	D	E	F	G	A	B	C	**Ionian** (major scale)
$\underline{II}$ - $\underline{II}$	D	E	F	G	A	B	C	D	**Dorian**
$\underline{III}$ - $\underline{III}$	E	F	G	A	B	C	D	E	**Phrygian**
$\underline{IV}$ - $\underline{IV}$	F	G	A	B	C	D	E	F	**Lydian**
$\underline{V}$ - $\underline{V}$	G	A	B	C	D	E	F	G	**Mixolydian**
$\underline{VI}$ - $\underline{VI}$	A	B	C	D	E	F	G	A	**Aeolian** (minor 'pure' scale)
$\underline{VII}$ - $\underline{VII}$	B	C	D	E	F	G	A	B	**Locrian**

Each of these modes will be most suited to a particular chord which occurs in the key. This relationship between the mode and the chord is summarized below.

MODE	CHORD	EXAMPLE (using key of C)		
$\bar{\text{I}}$ - $\bar{\text{I}}$	$\bar{\text{I}}$ maj7	C Ionian mode	matches	Cmaj7
$\bar{\text{II}}$ - $\bar{\text{II}}$	$\bar{\text{II}}$ m7	D Dorian mode	matches	Dm7
$\bar{\text{III}}$ - $\bar{\text{III}}$	$\bar{\text{III}}$ m7	E Phrygian mode	matches	Em7
$\bar{\text{IV}}$ - $\bar{\text{IV}}$	$\bar{\text{IV}}$ maj7	F Lydian mode	matches	Fmaj7
$\bar{\text{V}}$ - $\bar{\text{V}}$	$\bar{\text{V}}$ 7	G Mixolydian mode	matches	G7
$\bar{\text{VI}}$ - $\bar{\text{VI}}$	$\bar{\text{VI}}$ m7	A Aeolian mode	matches	Am7
$\bar{\text{VII}}$ - $\bar{\text{VII}}$	$\bar{\text{VII}}$ ø7	B Locrian mode	matches	Bø7

The following examples show how these modes can be used against a chord progression. Ex 72 illustrates the modes in relation to each chord, and ex 73 re-organizes them into a smooth, running lead line.

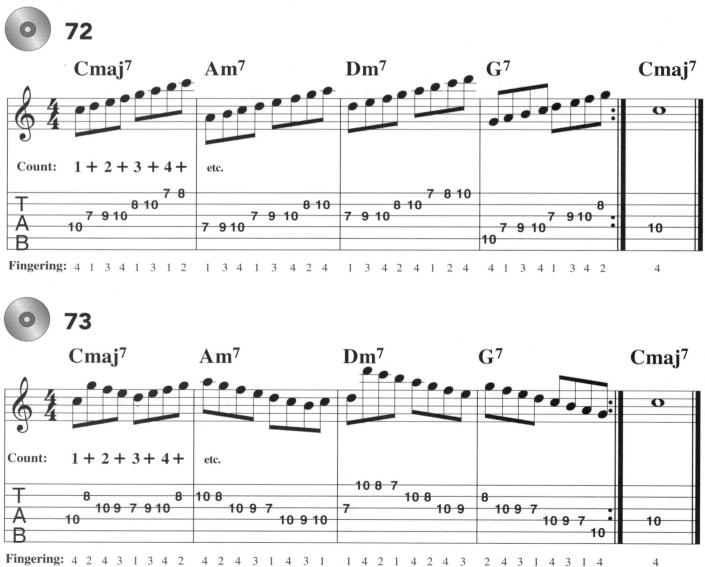

72

73

This concept of matching chords to scales can be taken much further than the brief outline given above. For a thorough study of scales and modes and their relationship to chords, see *Progressive Scales and Modes for Guitar*, and also the *Progressive Jazz Guitar* series.

APPENDIX ONE

MUSIC THEORY

This appendix will cover some essential areas of music theory that relate to the material studied in this book. All of the theory in this section should be thoroughly understood and learnt.

THE MAJOR SCALE

A scale can be defined as a series of notes in alphabetical order, progressing from any one note to its octave, and based upon a given set pattern. The pattern upon which the major scale is based is that of **tone - tone - semitone - tone - tone - tone - semitone**. E.g. starting on the C note and following through this pattern gives the C major scale.

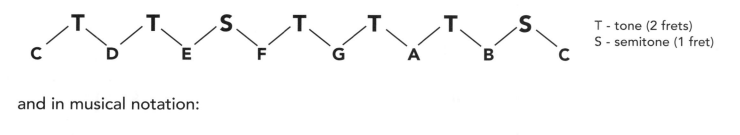

T - tone (2 frets)
S - semitone (1 fret)

and in musical notation:

C D E F G A B C

The major scale will always give the familiar sound of DO, RE, MI, FA, SO, LA, TI, DO.

It is important to remember that the major scale always uses the same pattern of tones and semitones, no matter what note is used as the tonic (starting note). Here are seven more major scales.

	T	T	S	T	T	T	S
G major:	G	A	B	C	D	E	F#	G
D major:	D	E	F#	G	A	B	C#	D
A major:	A	B	C#	D	E	F#	G#	A
E major:	E	F#	G#	A	B	C#	D#	E
F major:	F	G	A	B♭	C	D	E	F
B♭ major:	B♭	C	D	E♭	F	G	A	B♭
E♭ major:	E♭	F	G	A♭	B♭	C	D	E♭

KEY SIGNATURES

When music is talked of as being in a particular key, it means that the melody is based upon notes of the major scale with the same name, e.g. in the key of C, C major scale notes (i.e. C, D, E, F, G, A and B) will occur much more frequently than notes that do not belong to the C scale (i.e. sharpened and flattened notes).

In the key of G, G scale notes will be most common (i.e. the notes G, A, B, C, D, E and F# will occur frequently). You will notice here that F# occurs rather than F natural. However, rather than add a sharp to every F note, an easier method is used whereby a sharp sign is placed on the F line (the top one) of the staff at the beginning of each line. This is referred to as the **key signature**: thus the key signature of G major is F#.

Written below are the key signatures for all eight scales so far discussed.

C MAJOR

No sharps or flats

G MAJOR

F#

D MAJOR

F#, C#

A MAJOR

F#, C#, G#

E MAJOR

F#, C#, G#, D#

F MAJOR

B♭

B♭ MAJOR

B♭, E♭

E♭ MAJOR

B♭, E♭, A♭

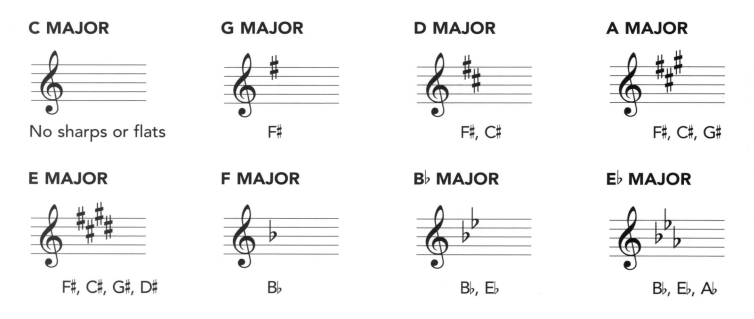

It can be seen, then, that each key signature is a shorthand representation of the scale, showing only the sharps or flats which occur in that scale. Where an additional sharp or flat occurs, it is not included as part of the key signature, but is written in the music, e.g. in the key of G, if a D# note occurs, the sharp sign will be written immediately before the D note, not at the beginning of the line as part of the key signature.

MINOR KEYS AND SCALES

Our discussion of major scales revealed that each key is based on a scale of the same name and that the key features the scale notes predominantly, e.g. the key of F major features the notes F, G, A, B♭, C, D and E. Many songs, however, are written in a minor key, which involves the use of minor scales. For each minor key, three minor scales exist. These three minor scales are written below, using the key of A minor as an example:

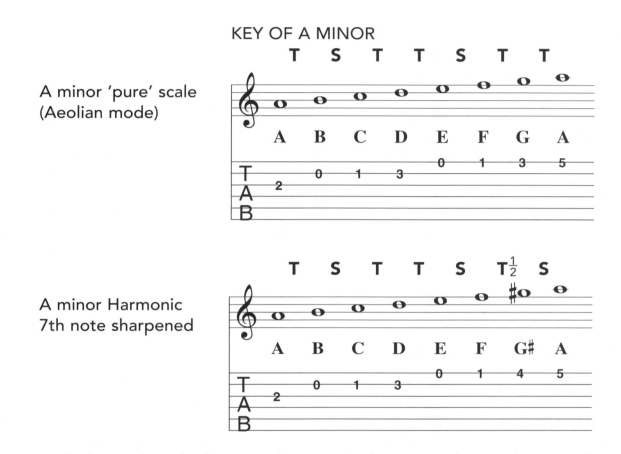

A minor Melodic – 6th and 7th notes sharpened when ascending and returned to natural when descending.

If you compare the A minor 'pure' scale with the C major scale you will notice that they contain the same notes (except starting on a different note). Because of this, these two scales are referred to as being 'relatives'; A minor is the relative minor of C major and vice versa.

For every major scale (and every major chord) there is a relative minor, as listed in the table below. On the guitar, relative minor chords can be located 3 frets down from the major chord. E.g. C major root 6 bar chord - 8th fret; A minor root 6 bar chord - 5th fret.

Major Key	C	Db	D	Eb	E	F	F#	G	Ab	A	Bb	B
Relative Minor Key	Am	Bbm	Bm	Cm	C#m	Dm	D#m	Em	Fm	F#m	Gm	G#m

The major key and its relative minor both share the same key signature, e.g. a key signature of F sharp could indicate either the key of G major, or the key of E minor. To determine the correct key, you can:

a) Look for the 7th note of the minor scale. This is the only note of a minor scale (except the 'pure' minor) which is not found in its relative major. E.g. a D# note in the melody will strongly suggest the key of E minor rather than G major.

b) Look at the finishing note of the piece, because a song very often finishes on its root note. E.g. a song finishing on a G note would suggest the key of G major. (Quite often the beginning and ending chords will also indicate the key in the same manner).

These are guidelines only and should not be taken as strict rules.

SCALE TONE CHORDS

In any given key certain chords are more common than others. E.g. in the key of C, the chords C, F and G are usually present, and quite often the chords Am, Dm and Em occur. The reason for this is that each key has its own set of chords, which are constructed from notes of its major scale. These chords are referred to as **scale tone chords**.

Consider the C major scale:

Chords are constructed by combining notes which are a third apart. For example, consider the formula for a major chord:

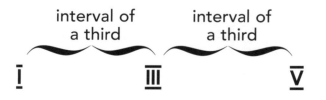

Using the C major scale written on the previous page, scale tone chords can be constructed by placing 2 third intervals above each note. This is illustrated in the table below:

$\underline{\bar{V}}$		G	A	B	C	D	E	F	G	} 3rd interval
$\underline{\overline{III}}$		E	F	G	A	B	C	D	E	} 3rd interval
C scale:		C	D	E	F	G	A	B	C	
Chord constructed:		**C**	**Dm**	**Em**	**F**	**G**	**Am**	**B°**	**C**	

Notice that the chords are named according to their root note (and hence the root note's scale). However, they are all C scale tone chords because they contain only notes of the C major scale (i.e. no sharps or flats). The method used for constructing scale tone chords in the key of C may be applied to any major scale. The result will always produce the following scale tone chords:

Scale note:	$\underline{\bar{I}}$	$\underline{\overline{II}}$	$\underline{\overline{III}}$	$\underline{\overline{IV}}$	$\underline{\bar{V}}$	$\underline{\overline{VI}}$	$\underline{\overline{VII}}$	$\underline{\overline{VIII}}$
Chord constructed:	**major**	**minor**	**minor**	**major**	**major**	**minor**	**diminished**	**major**

Thus in the key of G major, the scale tone chords will be:

| **G** | **Am** | **Bm** | **C** | **D** | **Em** | **F#°** | **G** |

and in the key of E♭ major, the scale tone chords will be:

| **E♭** | **Fm** | **Gm** | **A♭** | **B♭** | **Cm** | **D°** | **E♭** |

SCALE TONE CHORD EXTENSIONS

The scale tone chords studied so far involve the placement of two notes (separated by an interval of a third) above a root note. This method of building scale tone chords can be extended by adding another note, illustrated in the following table:

$\underline{\overline{VII}}$		B	C	D	E	F	G	A	B	} 3rd interval
$\underline{\bar{V}}$		G	A	B	C	D	E	F	G	} 3rd interval
$\underline{\overline{III}}$		E	F	G	A	B	C	D	E	} 3rd interval
C scale:		C	D	E	F	G	A	B	C	
Chord constructed:		**Cmaj7**	**Dm7**	**Em7**	**Fmaj7**	**G7**	**Am7**	**B°7***	**Cmaj7**	

From this example, the scale tone chords for any key will be:

$\underline{\bar{I}}$	$\underline{\overline{II}}$	$\underline{\overline{III}}$	$\underline{\overline{IV}}$	$\underline{\bar{V}}$	$\underline{\overline{VI}}$	$\underline{\overline{VII}}$	$\underline{\overline{VIII}}$
maj7	m7	m7	maj7	dom7	m7	°7	maj7

* This is called a half-diminished chord - °7

THE CHORD/KEY RELATIONSHIP

The chords which occur most frequently in any key will be those whose notes are taken from the key's major scale. E.g. in the key of C the most likely chords to appear will be those which contain all natural notes (i.e. notes from the C scale). Here are 25 such chords, which can be said to 'belong' to the key of C.

C	C6	Cmaj7	Cmaj9	Csus	Dm	Dm6	Dm7
($\underline{\text{I}}$)	($\underline{\text{I}}$6)	($\underline{\text{I}}$maj7)	($\underline{\text{I}}$maj9)	($\underline{\text{I}}$sus)	($\underline{\text{II}}$m)	($\underline{\text{II}}$m6)	($\underline{\text{II}}$m7)

Dm9	Em	Em7	F	F6	Fmaj7	Fmaj9	G
($\underline{\text{II}}$m9)	($\underline{\text{III}}$m)	($\underline{\text{III}}$m7)	($\underline{\text{IV}}$)	($\underline{\text{IV}}$6)	($\underline{\text{IV}}$maj7)	($\underline{\text{IV}}$maj9)	($\underline{\text{V}}$)

G6	G7	G9	G11	G13	Am	Am7	Am9	B°7
($\underline{\text{V}}$6)	($\underline{\text{V}}$7)	($\underline{\text{V}}$9)	($\underline{\text{V}}$11)	($\underline{\text{V}}$13)	($\underline{\text{VI}}$m)	($\underline{\text{VI}}$m7)	($\underline{\text{VI}}$m9)	($\underline{\text{VII}}$°7)

A thorough knowledge of these chords will help you decide the key of a piece (and therefore the location of improvising patterns) where no key signature is given. For example:

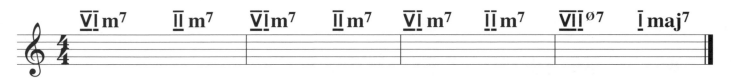

This progression is in the key of C, using the chords:

$$\underline{\text{VI}}\text{m}^7 \quad \underline{\text{II}}\text{m}^7 \quad \underline{\text{VI}}\text{m}^7 \quad \underline{\text{II}}\text{m}^7 \quad \underline{\text{VI}}\text{m}^7 \quad \underline{\text{II}}\text{m}^7 \quad \underline{\text{VII}}^{\varnothing 7} \quad \underline{\text{I}}\text{maj}^7$$

Another way to decide the key of a progression is to look at the first and last chords. These will often be the same, and also have the same name as the key. E.g. for a progression starting and finishing on F, the key is most likely to be F.

CHORD FORMULA CHART

The following chart lists chord formulas for the 8 most common keys used by lead guitarists. Other chords not listed can be derived by applying the correct formula to the respective scale; e.g.

B7 is based on the dom 7 formula ($\underline{\text{I}}$ - $\underline{\text{III}}$ - $\underline{\text{V}}$ - $\underline{\text{VII}}$) and the B scale:

Thus:	B	C#	D#	E	F#	G#	A#	B
	$\underline{\text{I}}$		$\underline{\text{III}}$		$\underline{\text{V}}$		♭$\underline{\text{VII}}$	
	B		D#		F#		A	

*The roman numerals written beneath each chord can be useful when transposing these 25 chords to other keys. Each roman numeral indicates the relative note of the major scale, e.g. in the key of C, $\underline{\text{I}}$ is C major, $\underline{\text{III}}$m is E minor etc. In the key of E, $\underline{\text{I}}$ is E major, $\underline{\text{III}}$m is G# minor etc.

CHORD FORMULA CHART

key	major	maj6	maj7	maj9	dom7	dom9	11	13
	1-3-5	1-3-5-6	1-3-5-7	1-3-5-7-9	1-3-5-b7	1-3-5-b7-9	1-3-5-b7-9-11	1-3-5-b7-9-13
C major No sharps or flats	C-E-G	C-E-G-A	C-E-G-B	C-E-G-B-D	C-E-G-Bb	C-E-G-Bb-D	C-E-G-Bb-D-F	C-E-G-Bb-D-A
G major F#	G-B-D	G-B-D-E	G-B-D-F#	G-B-D-F#-A	G-B-D-F	G-B-D-F-A	G-B-D-F-A-C	G-B-D-F-A-E
D major F#, C#	D-F#-A	D-F#-A-B	D-F#-A-C#	D-F#-A-C#-E	D-F#-A-C	D-F#-A-C-E	D-F#-A-C-E-G	D-F#-A-C-E-B
A major F#, C#, G#	A-C#-E	A-C#-E-F#	A-C#-E-G#	A-C#-E-G#-B	A-C#-E-G	A-C#-E-G-B	A-C#-E-G-B-D	A-C#-E-G-B-F#
E major F#, C#, G#, D#	E-G#-B	E-G#-B-C#	E-G#-B-D#	E-G#-B-D#-F#	E-G#-B-D	E-G#-B-D-F#	E-G#-B-D-F#-A	E-G#-B-D-F#-C#
F major Bb	F-A-C	F-A-C-D	F-A-C-E	F-A-C-E-G	F-A-C-Eb	F-A-C-Eb-G	F-A-C-Eb-G-Bb	F-A-C-Eb-G-D
Bb major Bb, Eb	Bb-D-F	Bb-D-F-G	Bb-D-F-A	Bb-D-F-A-C	Bb-D-F-Ab	Bb-D-F-Ab-C	Bb-D-F-Ab-C-Eb	Bb-D-F-Ab-C-G
Eb major Bb, Eb, Ab	Eb-G-Bb	Eb-G-Bb-C	Eb-G-Bb-D	Eb-G-Bb-D-F	Eb-G-Bb-Db	Eb-G-Bb-Db-F	Eb-G-Bb-Db-F-Ab	Eb-G-Bb-Db-F-C

key	minor	m6	m7	m9	augmented	half diminished7 (ø)	diminished7 (o)	suspended
	1-b3-5	1-b3-5-6	1-b3-5-b7	1-b3-5-b7-9	1-3-#5	1-b3-b5-b7	1-b3-b5-bb7	1-4-5
C major No sharps or flats	C-Eb-G	C-Eb-G-A	C-Eb-G-Bb	C-Eb-G-Bb-D	C-E-G#	C-Eb-Gb-Bb	C-Eb-Gb-Bbb	C-F-G
G major F#	G-Bb-D	G-Bb-D-E	G-Bb-D-F	G-Bb-D-F-A	G-B-D#	G-Bb-Db-F	G-Bb-Db-Fb	G-C-D
D major F#, C#	D-F-A	D-F-A-B	D-F-A-C	D-F-A-C-E	D-F#-A#	D-F-Ab-C	D-F-Ab-Cb	D-G-A
A major F#, C#, G#	A-C-E	A-C-E-F#	A-C-E-G	A-C-E-G-B	A-C#-E#	A-C-Eb-G	A-C-Eb-Gb	A-D-E
E major F#, C#, G#, D#	E-G-B	E-G-B-C#	E-G-B-D	E-G-B-D-F#	E-G#-B#	E-G-Bb-D	E-G-Bb-Db	E-A-B
F major Bb	F-Ab-C	F-Ab-C-D	F-Ab-C-Eb	F-Ab-C-Eb-G	F-A-C#	F-Ab-Cb-Eb	F-Ab-Cb-Ebb	F-Bb-C
Bb major Bb, Eb	Bb-Db-F	Bb-Db-F-G	Bb-Db-F-Ab	Bb-Db-F-Ab-C	Bb-D-F#	Bb-Db-Fb-Ab	Bb-Db-Fb-Abb	Bb-Eb-F
Eb major Bb, Eb, Ab	Eb-Gb-Bb	Eb-Gb-Bb-C	Eb-Gb-Bb-Db	Eb-Gb-Bb-Db-F	Eb-G-B	Eb-Gb-Bbb-Db	Eb-Gb-Bbb-Dbb	Eb-Ab-Bb

APPENDIX TWO

IMPROVISING WITHIN A SONG

Improvising within a song involves special considerations which are not necessary when just 'jamming' with a chord progression. These considerations are most important when you reach the stage of forming a repertoire for group performance.

In a song, the lead guitarist does not usually play at the same time as the singer is singing. (When a lead guitarist is not playing lead, they generally play rhythm). Instead he or she may play 'fill-ins' in between the singers lines, or play a lead solo during a vocal break. Another common role for the lead guitarist is to play a brief introduction or ending to the song.

INTRODUCTIONS

An introduction will often involve a short (4 or 8 bars) musical phrase. This 'riff' is designed to attract the attention of the listener and help make the song instantly recognizable and memorable. It may be repeated throughout the song (e.g. during the lead break, or at the end of the song). The melody of the introduction is usually played against the chord progression of the song, or some part of it (e.g. it may be based on the chords used in the verses, chorus or bridge). The riff may also 'borrow' the melody of either the verses or chorus.

FILL-INS

A fill-in is a short lead riff played between one line of the lyric and the next; or between one verse and the next etc. This is the period where the singer usually holds a long note or has a small break. Any of the licks you have studied so far could be used as a fill-in.

LEAD SOLOS

A lead solo involves the lead guitarist playing for a full verse or chorus of the song (or longer), while the singer has a rest. It may occur at the beginning or end of the song, but is more commonly found either half way or two-thirds of the way through the song. There are three basic levels of relationship between a lead solo and the melody line.

Level One -   The lead solo consisting of an exact repeat of the melody (sometimes an octave higher for clarity). This occurs quite often in commercial 'pop' songs where the lead break is relatively short.

Level Two -   The lead solo being based on the melody, but having noticeable changes (e.g. in timing variations, extra notes added, and the use of techniques such as bends and slurs).

Level Three-   The lead solo being completely different from the melody (this often applies to Rock songs, where the solo may last for a considerable length of time).

IDEAS FOR IMPROVISING

When you hear lead solos on record, most of them are not improvised, but instead have been worked out in advance. In such examples, the lead solo is said to be composed, rather than improvised (in 'live' group performances, however, there is likely to be more improvising involved, as lead solos are often extended).

One of the main aims in improvising is to create variety and listed below are some ideas to achieve this.

1.   Techniques (slurs, slides, tremolos, bends, etc).

2.   Short 'catchy' riffs. These may be melodic in nature, or scale-like.

3.   Variation in timing, e.g. triplets, rests, speed variations, syncopation (accenting the 'off' beat) etc.

4.   Dynamics (loud and soft variations) including staccato (short and detached), legato (smooth) and accents (highlighting a note).

5.   Scale runs (usually fast) and melodic passages.

6.   Harmony notes - 3rds, 6ths and octaves. Also the use of three or four string chords (usually played on the first 4 strings).

7.   Additional notes and passing notes.

8.   Controls on the guitar, e.g. volume, tone controls, pick-up switch and tremolo arm (if fitted).

9.   Controls on the amplifier, e.g. volume, tone, reverb, tremolo, harmonic balance, distortion etc.

10.   Electronic effects (i.e. gadgets) such as the distortion box, echo units, phasers, wah-wah and volume pedals etc. These gadgets will add an extra dimension to your playing and enable you to achieve more accurately the sounds you hear on record.

The best way to develop your improvising ability is to play with other musicians as much as possible. If you are jamming with another guitarist, you can take turns at playing lead and rhythm. When you are playing rhythm, listen to the lead player and try to provide a solid base for them to improvise over. When your turn comes to play lead, see if you can use some of the ideas of the other player and alter them to create your own licks. Playing along with records is another valuable way of developing your improvisation skills. When you improvise a solo, try to play something that makes sense in relation to what has gone before it and where you are going next. Playing a solo should be like telling a story rather than a series of unrelated licks. Listen to players you admire and try to work out what makes them sound the way they do. Most of the great lead players have learned a lot by copying licks and solos from records and then developed their own style from what they have learned. Copying solos from recordings is dealt with in appendix four.

APPENDIX THREE

MODULATION

Modulation can be defined as the changing of key within a song (or chord progression). It is very important to recognize a modulation, should it occur, and adjust the fret location of each pattern accordingly.

In sheet music, a modulation is sometimes indicated by changing the key signature. This will usually be done if the modulation occurs between one section of the song and the next (e.g. between one verse and another). Where there is no change of key signature, a modulation may be detected by examining the melody and/or the chords. When examining the melody, remember that each key is recognizable by the notes of its scale. If different notes appear it may indicate a modulation. E.g. if a melody in the key of C suddenly features F♯ notes, it could suggest a modulation to the key of G. When examining the chords, a modulation may be determined by following the chord/key relationship, i.e. looking for chords that 'fit in' to a certain key. Consider the following progression:

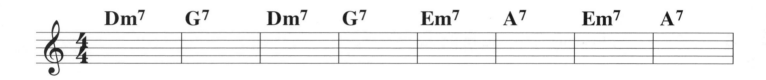

which can be analyzed as such:

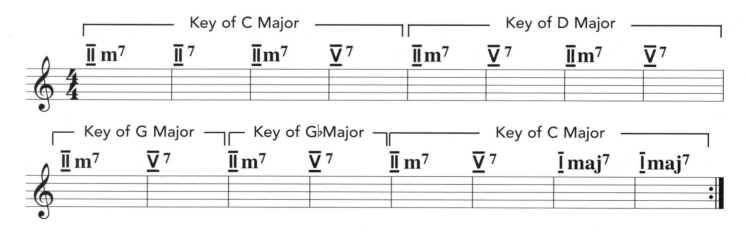

The use of Roman numerals makes the lay-out of this progression very clear, it is based on the $\overline{II}$m7 - $\overline{V}$7 chords, modulating through four different keys. This type of modulation is most common in Jazz songs. You will find that many Rock songs, although featuring modulation, will not do so to such a great extent.

One of the most common modulations in songs is from the major key to its relative minor:

No change of pattern is necessary in this situation, however, different notes should be emphasized, i.e. when modulating to the relative minor key (A minor), the new root note (A) should be emphasized.

Another common form of modulation is to change up to the key one semitone or one tone higher. This can be done successively, as in the following example:

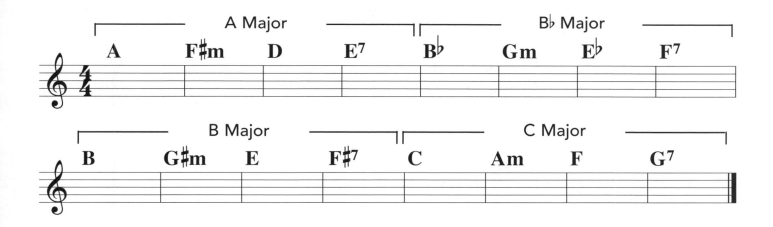

When a modulation occurs, your patterns will change fret accordingly. For example, if a major key chord progression modulates through the following keys: C – G – F – C then the fret location of pattern one will change as such:

KEY:	C	G	F	C
Pattern:	5th	12th	10th	5th

However, it is not necessary to change positions; instead you can change patterns to avoid uncomfortable 'jumps' up and down the neck. E.g. consider the use of three patterns:

KEY:	C	G	F	C
Pattern:	1	3	4	1
Fret Location:	5th	5th	5th	5th

Hence you are able to change key with minimal position changes.

APPENDIX FOUR

EAR TRAINING

In improvising it is most desirable to hear a lead line 'in your head' and then be able to translate it immediately to the fretboard. The following points will give you some guidelines for developing this ability.

1.   Play a scale (e.g. the major scale) very slowly through one octave. As you do so, sing aloud each note. You should sing the note immediately after you play it. Continue doing this until you feel confident that you are singing each note correctly.

2.   Play the root note of the scale. Sing the next note and then play it to check your pitch. Proceed through the rest of the scale in the same manner; singing each note and then playing it.

3.   Play the root note of a scale and sing through the scale with no reinforcement until the octave note is reached.

4.   Play the root note of a scale and then name another note of that scale and sing it, e.g. using the C major scale, play the C note and sing the A note. To help you remember these intervals, pick a song you know which uses them (e.g. C to A are the first two notes of "My Bonnie Lies Over the Ocean".

5.   Play 'around' the notes of a scale, firstly singing each note just after you play it; and then singing each note before it is played. Do this very slowly at first. At this point you are pre-hearing melody notes.

6.   Sing melodies of songs that you know and play them as you do so. Do the same with lead lines.

7.   Sing chord arpeggios. Experiment with different chord types (e.g. major, minor, dominant 7th etc) and try some inversions (e.g. starting on the third or fifth of the chord, instead of the first).

8.   Sing chromatic notes (i.e. notes that are a semitone apart). If you can sing a scale correctly, try adding passing notes.

Another useful ear training exercise is to get together with another musician and play 'call and response' (sometimes called question and answer). This involves one player playing a line and the other player imitating it immediately, either exactly or almost exactly. Try doing this with no set time at first, when it becomes easier, try using a metronome or drum machine set to a slow tempo. Gradually increase the tempo once you are comfortable with the process. This type of exercise is a lot of fun and is also valuable training for a band situation where you are required to play the responses as fill-ins between vocal phrases. Call and response is a particularly strong element in Blues and other African American music such as Gospel, Soul and Funk. For a more in-depth look at call and response style playing, see *Progressive Blues Guitar Licks* and *Progressive Funk and R&B Guitar Method*.

COPYING LEAD SOLOS FROM RECORDS

As a lead guitarist, you will sometimes be required to play a given lead solo from a recording (as compared to composing one, or just improvising). This can be very difficult, particularly at first, so here are a few suggestions:

1. Your guitar should **always** be tuned to concert pitch (this occurs when the A note on the first string at the 5th fret vibrates at 440 cycles per second). Check with an electronic tuner, tuning fork, pitch pipes or a piano. This is necessary because all recorded music is at concert pitch.

2. Start with a simple lead solo. Tape it onto a cassette so that you can play it many times over easily.

3. Listen carefully to the rhythm of the notes and determine the time signature of the piece. Once this is done, you can break the solo into smaller phrases, or even down to one bar at a time.

4. Sing through the phrase and then try to locate those notes on the guitar.

5. As you work through the solo, try to determine the key of the piece. This should help you to anticipate the notes as they come and perhaps locate a pattern into which they fall. E.g. if you are working on a solo which contains C#s and F#s, this will suggest the key of D major. You may then find that the solo fits in with one of the major pentatonic patterns in this key.

6. With faster solos it is beneficial to use a tape recorder where the speed can be reduced by half on playback. This also lowers the pitch of the notes by one octave, so you will have to compensate accordingly.

7. Practice record copying (often referred to as 'transcribing') regularly, but not for a long period of time in each session, as your concentration and hearing ability declines.

LISTENING

As well as transcribing solos, you will need to do a lot of listening to lead guitarists to learn what type of playing sounds best in each musical situation. Since all lead guitarists use the same notes, it is the way they put these notes together, along with the phrasing and timing they use that makes one player sound different from the next. Listen to albums featuring different lead players and try to notice what it is that makes each player sound the way they do. It may be a particular way of bending notes, a way of playing around with the timing, the use of dynamics, a particular vibrato sound, or a combination of many elements. Listen analytically to solos and figure out what you like and what you don't like. Try to copy the aspects you do like and then experiment with them to create your own style. It is very useful to listen to players from older styles of music, particularly Blues, as most of the techniques, sounds and musical language used by all lead guitarists were pioneered by Blues players such as T-Bone Walker and B.B. King. Some other great Blues players include Albert Collins, Otis Rush, Buddy Guy, Magic Sam, Gatemouth Brown, Peter Green (early Fleetwood Mac), Eric Clapton, Stevie Ray Vaughan, Debbie Davies and Gary Moore. For open string slur sounds it is useful to listen to Rock players such as Angus Young (ACDC), Ritchie Blackmore (Deep Purple) and Eddie Van Halen who is also the originator of the two handed tapping style.

APPENDIX FIVE

HARMONICS

A harmonic is a chime like sound created by lightly touching a vibrating string at certain points along the fretboard.

NATURAL HARMONICS

A natural harmonic is produced by lightly touching an open string at either the 12th, 7th, 5th or 19th frets, while picking it.* Harmonics must be played directly over the fret and should just touch the string, not push it down.

Playing harmonics on the 12th fret of the first string.

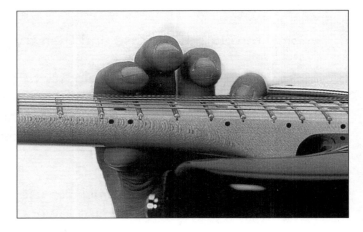

To play harmonics, use the underside of your first finger.

Harmonics are indicated by diamond shaped notes as such:

*Harmonics can be located at other frets, but these are the most common.

On the 12th fret, the harmonics produced have the same pitch as the fretted note on the same string.

e.g. first string, 12th fret note (E)   first string, 12th fret harmonic (E)

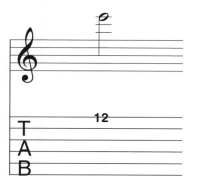 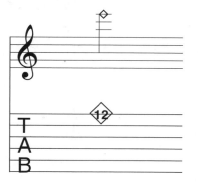

On the 7th fret, the harmonics produced are an octave higher than the fretted note on the same string.

e.g. fifth string, 7th fret note (E)   fifth string, 7th fret harmonic (E)

On the 19th fret, the harmonics produced have the same pitch as the fretted note on the same string. These harmonics are also identical to the harmonics produced on the 7th fret.

On the 5th fret, the harmonics produced are an octave and a fifth higher than the fretted note on the same string.

e.g. fourth string, 5th fret note (G)   fourth string, 5th fret harmonic (D)

 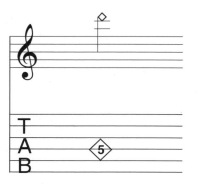

The table below sets out the note names of harmonics produced on the 5th, 7th, 12th and 19th frets;

TABLE OF NATURAL HARMONICS

STRING	5th	7th	12th	19th
E(6th)	E	B	E	B
A	A	E	A	E
D	D	A	D	A
G	G	D	G	D
B	B	F#	B	F#
E	E	B	E	B

In this table, the harmonics produced on the 7th and 19th frets are identical, however, the harmonics produced on the 5th fret are an octave higher than those on the 12th fret.

TUNING BY HARMONICS

Harmonics are commonly used as a method to tune the guitar. By locating harmonics of the same pitch on different strings, you can tune the guitar as such:

STRING	5th FRET	7th FRET
6	E ←1	B
5	A ←2	E
4	D ←3	A
3	G	D
2	B	F#
1	E	B

1. Tune the harmonic on the 7th fret of the fifth string to the harmonic on the 5th fret of the sixth string (arrow 1).

2. Tune the harmonic on the 7th fret of the fourth string to the harmonic on the 5th fret of the fifth string (arrow 2).

3. Tune the harmonic on the 7th fret of the third string to the harmonic on the 5th fret of the fourth string (arrow 3).

4. Tune the open second string to the harmonic on the 7th fret of the sixth string.

5. Tune the open first string to the harmonic on the 7th fret of the fifth string.

ARTIFICIAL HARMONICS

Whereas natural harmonics are played with open strings, artificial harmonics are played by lightly touching a string at a point one octave higher than a given fretted note. For example, if an A note is played on the 2nd fret of the third string, an artificial harmonic can be played at the 14th fret on the same string (i.e. one octave higher). Use the middle finger of your right hand and tap the string lightly to produce the harmonic. Add volume, treble and distortion to enhance the sound of the artificial harmonic.

There is also another right hand technique used to produce artificial harmonics which is shown below. The picking hand grips the pick between the thumb and the middle finger, leaving the index finger free (see photo).

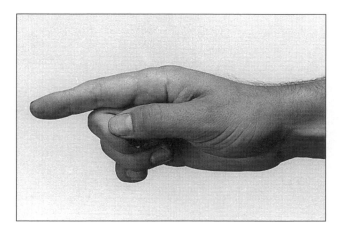

The index finger touches the string 12 frets above the fretted note, while the pick attacks the string. The picking action is initiated by movement in the thumb knuckle.

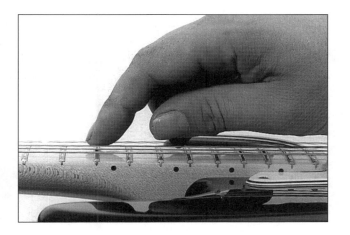 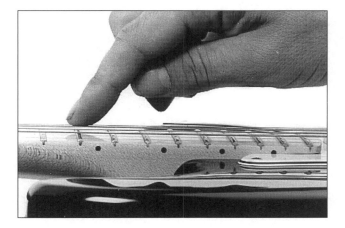

Artificial Harmonic Picking Technique

Artificial harmonics can be played with any fretted note, by touching the string one octave (12 frets) higher. Other artificial harmonics can be located 5 and 7 frets above the fretted note (e.g. for the A note previously mentioned, artificial harmonics are at the 7th and 9th frets, as well as the 14th. For a more detailed look at the use of harmonics on electric guitar, see *Progressive Heavy Metal Techniques for Lead Guitar*. For solos including harmonics on acoustic guitar, see *Progressive Fingerpicking Guitar Solos*.

APPENDIX SIX

CHORD PROGRESSIONS

The following chord progressions* have been selected to help you practice Blues, major key and minor key improvising.

BLUES AND ROCK PROGRESSIONS

*All chord shapes can be found in *Progressive Rhythm Guitar* by Gary Turner and Brenton White.

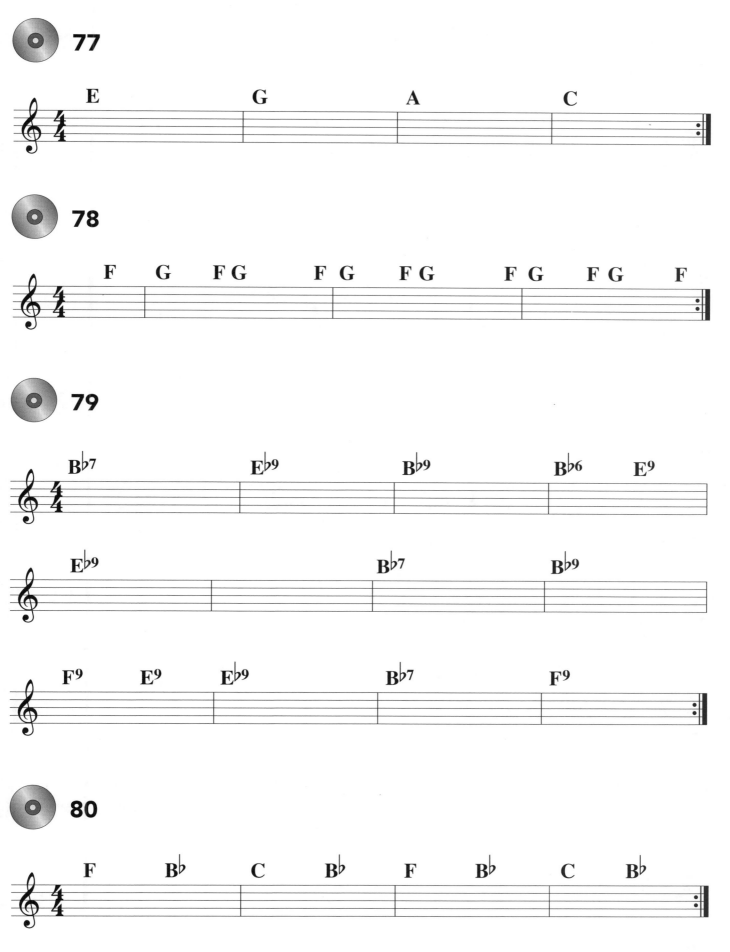

MAJOR KEY PROGRESSIONS

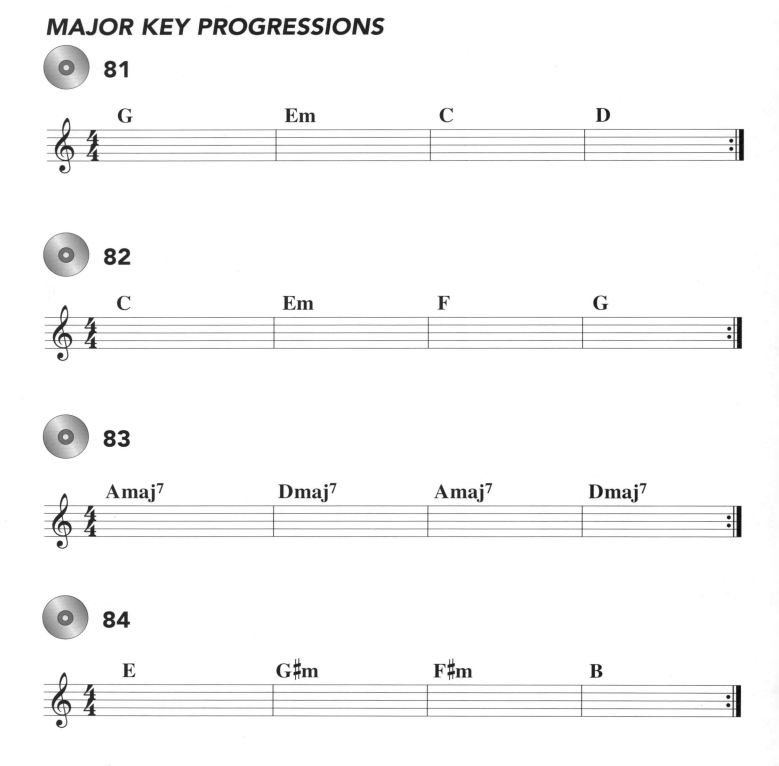

81

G   Em   C   D

82

C   Em   F   G

83

$Amaj^7$ $Dmaj^7$ $Amaj^7$ $Dmaj^7$

84

E   G♯m   F♯m   B

You will notice that the following progression has also been included in the 'Blues' progressions listed on the previous page. As outlined in lesson 13, many progressions in a major key can also be treated as a "Blues" when improvising.

85

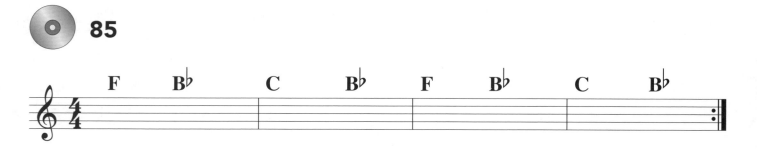

F B♭   C B♭   F B♭   C B♭

MINOR KEY PROGRESSIONS

87

88

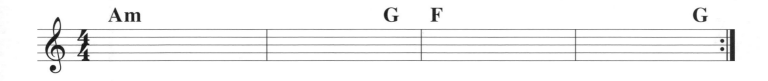

89

96

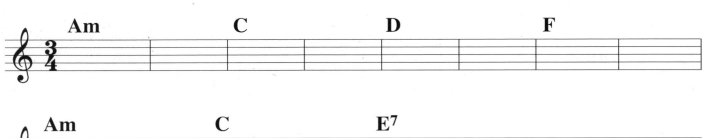

90

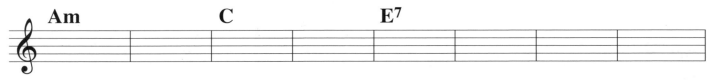

91

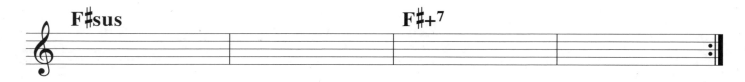

MODULATION

 **92**

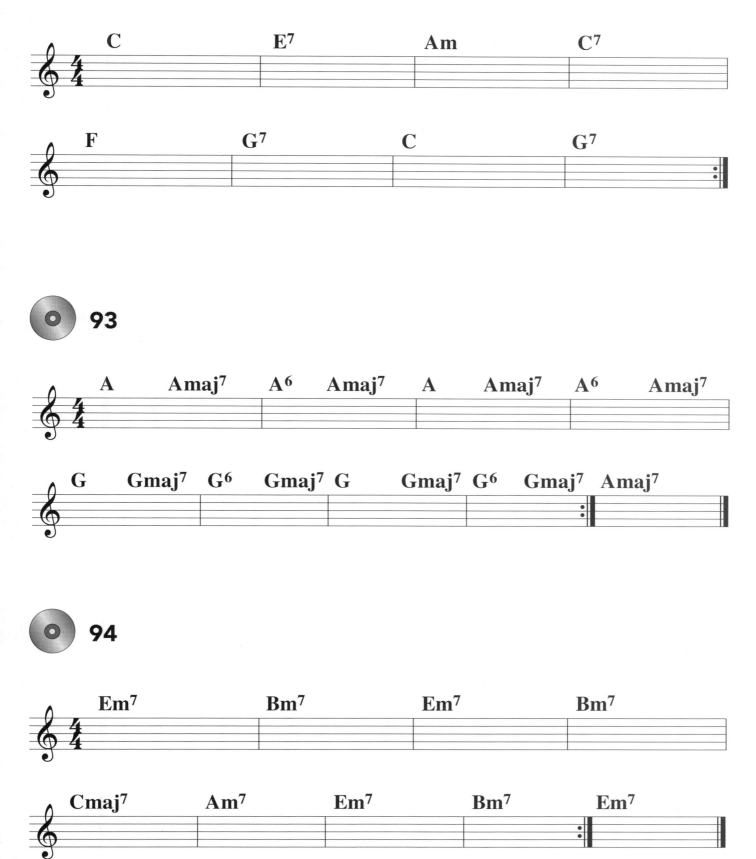

GLOSSARY OF MUSICAL TERMS

'a' – annular finger (ring finger). As used for identifying the right hand fingers in fingerpicking patterns.

Accent — a sign, > used to indicate a predominant note or beat.

Accidental — a sign used to show a temporary change in pitch of a note (i.e. sharp ♯, flat ♭, double sharp ✗, double flat ♭♭, or natural ♮). The sharps or flats in a key signature are not regarded as accidentals.

Additional notes — a note not belonging to a given scale, but can be used for improvising against most notes in a progression without sounding out of key.

Ad lib — to be played at the performer's own discretion.

Allegretto — moderately fast.

Allegro — fast and lively.

Anacrusis — a note or notes occurring before the first bar of music (also called 'lead-in' notes).

Andante — an easy walking pace.

Arpeggio — the playing of a chord in single note fashion.

Bar — a division of music occurring between two bar lines (also called a 'measure').

Bar chord — a chord played with one finger lying across all six strings.

Bar line — a vertical line drawn across the staff which divides the music into equal sections called bars.

Bass — the lower regions of pitch in general. On guitar, the 4th, 5th and 6th strings.

Bend — a technique which involves pushing a string upwards (or downward), which raises the pitch of the fretted note being played.

Blues Scale — consisting of the $\bar{\text{I}}$, ♭$\overline{\text{III}}$, $\overline{\text{IV}}$, ♭$\overline{\text{V}}$, $\overline{\text{V}}$ and ♭$\overline{\text{VII}}$ notes relative to the major scale.

Capo — a device placed across the neck of a guitar to allow a key change without alteration of the chord shapes.

Chord — a combination of three or more different notes played together.

Chord progression — a series of chords played as a musical unit (e.g. as in a song).

Chromatic scale — a scale ascending and descending in semitones.
e.g. **C** chromatic scale:

ascending:	C	C♯	D	D♯	E	F	F♯	G	G♯	A	A♯	B	C
descending:	C	B	B♭	A	A♭	G	G♭	F	E	E♭	D	D♭	C

Clef — a sign placed at the beginning of each staff of music which fixes the location of a particular note on the staff, and hence the location of all other notes, e.g.

Treble Staff   Bass Staff

Coda — an ending section of music, signified by the sign $\oplus$.

Common time — and indication of $\frac{4}{4}$ time — four quarter note beats per bar (also indicated by $\mathbf{C}$)

Compound time — occurs when the beat falls on a dotted note, which is thus divisible by 3 e.g. $\frac{6}{8}$ $\frac{9}{8}$ $\frac{12}{8}$

D.C al fine — a repeat from the beginning to the word 'fine'.

Dot — a sign placed after a note indicating that its time value is extended by a half. e.g.

$\downarrow$ = 2 counts $\downarrow.$ = 2 counts

Double Bar Line — two vertical lines close together, indicating the end of a piece, or section thereof.

Double Flat — a sign ($\flat\flat$) which lowers the pitch of a note by one tone.

Double Sharp — a sign ($\times$) which raises the pitch of a note by one tone.

D.S. al fine — a repeat from the sign (indicated thus $\%$) to the word 'fine'.

Duration — the time value of each note.

Dynamics — the varying degrees of softness (indicated by the term 'piano') and loudness (indicated by the term 'forte') in music.

Eighth note — a note with the value of half a beat in $\frac{4}{4}$ time, indicated thus $\eighthnote$ (also called a quaver).

The eighth note rest, indicating half a beat of silence is written: γ

Enharmonic — describes the difference in notation, but not in pitch, of two notes: e.g.

F# and G♭:

Fermata — a sign, $\frown$, used to indicate that a note or chord is held to the player's own discretion (also called a 'pause sign').

Fill in — a short lead riff played between one line of a lyric and the next, or between one verse and the next.

First and second endings — signs used where two different endings occur. On the first time through ending one is played (indicated by the bracket ⌐1　　　⌐); then the progression is repeated and ending two is played (indicated ⌐2　　　).

Flat — a sign, ($\flat$)used to lower the pitch of a note by one semitone.

Form — the plan or layout of a song, in relation to the sections it contains; e.g. Binary form, containing an "A" section and a "B" section (AB).
Ternary form, containing an A section and a B section, and then a repeat of the A section (ABA).
The verse/chorus relationship in songs is an example of form.

Forte — loud. Indicated by the sign f .

Free stroke — where the finger, after picking the string, does not come to rest on any other string (as used in fingerpicking.

Half note — a note with the value of two beats in $\frac{4}{4}$ time, indicated thus: $\downarrow$ (also called a minim).
The half note rest, indicating two beats of silence, is written: ▬ ← third staff line.

Hammer on — sounding a note by using only the left hand fingers (also called a 'slur').

Harmonics — a chime like sound created by lightly touching a vibrating string at certain points along the fret board.

Harmony — the simultaneous sounding of two or more different notes.

'i' — index finger. As used for identifying the right hand fingers in fingerpicking patterns.

Improvise — to perform spontaneously; i.e. not from memory or from a written copy.

Interval — the distance between any two notes of different pitches.

Key — describes the notes used in a composition in regards to the major or minor scale from which they are taken; e.g. a piece 'in the key of C major' describes the melody, chords, etc., as predominantly consisting of the notes, **C, D, E, F, G, A,** and **B** — i.e. from the **C** scale.

Key signature — a sign, placed at the beginning of each stave of music, directly after the clef, to indicate the key of a piece. The sign consists of a certain number of sharps or flats, which represent the sharps or flats found in the scale of the piece's key. e.g.

 indicates a scale with F♯ and C♯, which is D major; D E F♯ G A B C♯ D. Therefore the key is D major.

Lead-In — same as anacrusis (also called a pick-up).

Leger lines — small horizontal lines upon which notes are written when their pitch is either above or below the range of the staff, e.g.

Legato — smoothly, well connected.

Lyric — words that accompany a melody.

'm' — middle finger. As used for identifying the right hand fingers in fingerpicking patterns.

Major Pentatonic Scale — a 5 tone scale based on the interval sequence, T, T, T$\frac{1}{2}$, T, T$\frac{1}{2}$.

Major Scale — a series of eight notes in alphabetical order based on the interval sequence tone - tone - semitone - tone - tone - tone - semitone, giving the familiar sound **do re mi fa so la ti do.**

Melody — a succession of notes of varying pitch and duration, and having a recognizable musical shape.

Metronome — a device which indicates the number of beats per minute, and which can be adjusted in accordance to the desired tempo.
e.g. **MM** (Maelzel Metronome) ♩ = 60 — indicates 60 quarter note beats per minute.

Minor Pentatonic Scale — a 5 tone scale based on the interval sequence, T$\frac{1}{2}$, T, T, T$\frac{1}{2}$, T.

Mode — a displaced scale e.g. playing through the C to C scale, but starting and finishing on the D note.

Moderato — at a moderate pace.

Modulation — the changing of key within a song (or chord progression).

Natural — a sign (♮)used to cancel our the effect of a sharp or flat. The word is also used to describe the notes **A, B, C, D, E, F** and **G**; e.g. 'the natural notes'.

Notation — the written representation of music, by means of symbols (music on a staff), letters (as in chord and note names) and diagrams (as in chord illustrations.)

Note — a single sound with a given pitch and duration.

Octave — the distance between any given note with a set frequency, and another note with exactly double that frequency. Both notes will have the same letter name;

Open chord — a chord that contains at least one open string.

'p' — primary finger (thumb). As used for identifying the right hand fingers in fingerpicking patterns.

Passing note — connects two melody notes which are a third or less apart. A passing note usually occurs on an unaccented beat of the bar.

Phrase — a small group of notes forming a recognizable unit within a melody.

Pivot finger — a finger which remains in position while the other fingers move, when changing chords.

Pitch — the sound produced by a note, determined by the frequency of the string vibrations. The pitch relates to a note being referred to as 'high' or 'low'.

Plectrum — a small object (often of a triangular shape) made of plastic which is used to pick or strum the strings of a guitar.

Position — a term used to describe the location of the left hand on the fret board. The left hand position is determined by the fret location of the first finger, e.g.
The 1st position refers to the 1st to 4th frets. The 3rd position refers to the 3rd to 6th frets and so on.

Quarter note — a note with the value of one beat in $\frac{4}{4}$ time, indicated thus ♩ (also called a crotchet). The quarter note rest, indicating one beat of silence, is written: 𝄽 .

Relative — a term used to describe the relationship between a major and minor key which share the same key signature; e.g. G major and E minor are relative keys both sharing the F♯ key signature.

Repeat signs — in music, used to indicate a repeat of a section of music, by means of two dots placed before a double bar line:

In chord progressions, a repeat sign ✗ , indicates and exact repeat of the previous bar.

Rest — the notation of an absence of sound in music.

Rest stroke — where the finger, after picking the string, comes to rest on the next string (for accenting the note).

Rhythm — the note after which a chord or scale is named (also called 'key note').

Riff — a pattern of notes that is repeated throughout a progression (song).

Root note — the note after which a chord or scale is named (also called 'key note').
Scale Tone Chords — chords which are constructed from notes within a given scale.

Semitone — the smallest interval used in conventional music. On guitar, it is a distance of one fret.

Sharp — a sign (♯) used to raise the pitch of a note by one semitone.

Simple time — occurs when the beat falls on an undotted note, which is thus divisible by two.

Sixteenth note — a note with the value of quarter of a beat in $\frac{4}{4}$ time, indicated thus ♬ (also called a semiquaver).
The sixteenth note rest, indicating quarter of a beat of silence, is written: 𝄿

Slide — a technique which involves a finger moving along the string to its new note. The finger maintains pressure on the string, so that a continuous sound is produced.

Slur — sounding a note by using only the left hand fingers. (An ascending slur is also called 'hammer-on'; a descending slur is also called 'pull-off')

Staccato — to play short and detached. Indicated by a dot placed above the note:

Staff — five parallel lines together with four spaces, upon which music is written.

Syncopation — the placing of an accent on a normally unaccented beat. e.g.:

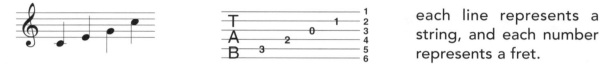

Tablature — a system of writing music which represents the position of the player's fingers (not the pitch of the notes, but their position on the guitar). A chord diagram is a type of tablature. Notes can also be written using tablature thus:

each line represents a string, and each number represents a fret.

Tempo — the speed of a piece.

Tie — a curved line joining two or more notes of the same pitch, where the second note(s) is not played, but its time value is added to that of the first note.

In example two, the first note is held for seven counts.

Timbre — a quality which distinguishes a note produced on one instrument from the same note produced on any other instrument (also called 'tone colour'). A given note on the guitar will sound different (and therefore distinguishable) from the same pitched note on piano, violin, flute etc. There is usually also a difference in timbre from one guitar to another.

Time signature — a sign at the beginning of a piece which indicates, by means of figures, the number of beats per bar (top figure), and the type of note receiving one beat (bottom figure).

Tone — a distance of two frets; i.e. the equivalent of two semitones.

Transposition — the process of changing music from one key to another.

Treble — the upper regions of pitch in general.

Treble clef — a sign placed at the beginning of the staff to fix the pitch of the notes placed on it. The treble clef (also called 'G clef') is placed so that the second line indicates as G note:

Tremolo (pick tremolo) — a technique involving rapid pick movement on a given note.

Triplet — a group of three notes played in the same time as two notes of the same kind.

Eighth note triplet

Vibrato — a technique which involves pushing a string up and down, like a rapid series of short bends.

Whole note — a note with the value of four beats in $\frac{4}{4}$ time, indicated thus **o** (also called a semibreve). The whole note rest, indicating four beats of silence, is written: ⟵ 4th staff line.

PROGRESSIVE SCALES AND MODES FOR GUITAR
FOR BEGINNER TO ADVANCED

Progressive Scales and Modes gives the student a complete system for learning any scale, mode or chord and makes it easy to memorize any new new sound as well as building a solid visual and aural foundation of both the theory and the guitar fretboard. The book also shows you how to use each scale as well as how and why it fits with a particular chord or progression. The final section contains jam along progressions for every scale and mode presented in the book.

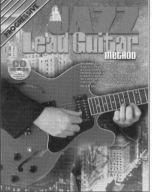

PROGRESSIVE JAZZ LEAD GUITAR METHOD
BEGINNER TO INTERMEDIATE

A great introduction to Jazz lead guitar playing. Demonstrates all the essential rhythms, scales, modes and arpeggios needed to become a good Jazz player. Also deals with playing over chord changes, improvising and Blues playing. Each new technique or concept is consolidated with at least one full-length solo.

PROGRESSIVE LEAD GUITAR LICKS
FOR BEGINNER TO ADVANCED

Features over 110 licks incorporating the styles and techniques used by the world's best lead guitarists. Covers Rock, Blues, Metal, Country, Jazz, Funk, Soul, Rockabilly, Slide and Fingerpicking. Several solos are included to fully show how the licks and techniques can be used to create a lead guitar solo. The emphasis in this volume is to provide a vast variety of music styles to enable you to fit in with any music or recording situation. All licks are clearly notated using standard music notation and 'Easy Read' guitar tab.

PROGRESSIVE ROCK GUITAR LICKS
FOR INTERMEDIATE TO ADVANCED

This book may be used by itself or as a useful supplement to *Progressive Rock Guitar Technique*. The licks throughout the book are examples of how the most popular lead guitar patterns can be used in all positions on the fretboard, and how various techniques can be applied to each pattern. Several Rock guitar solos are included to fully show how the licks and techniques studied throughout the book can be used to create a solo.

PROGRESSIVE SLIDE GUITAR TECHNIQUE
FOR BEGINNER TO ADVANCED

A comprehensive, easy to follow guide, introducing all the important techniques required to play slide guitar. Including: damping, fretting, sliding, vibrato, slide scales and open tunings. Concentrates on the use of slide in modern Rock and Blues styles. This book is particularly useful to modern guitar players who wish to incorporate slide into an electric Rock and Blues style. Contains many techniques, licks and solos as well as valuable information on types of slides and guitars as well as setting up a guitar for slide playing.

PROGRESSIVE METAL GUITAR METHOD
BEGINNER TO ADVANCED

Covers all the basics of Metal guitar playing in a clear, easy to follow method. Covers both rhythm and lead and introduces essential techniques such as hammer-ons, pull-offs, slides, bends and tapping. Also demonstrates essential scales, chords, rhythms and timing, along with theory as it relates to metal guitar playing. Contains lots of great sounding licks and solos and many classic metal sounds.

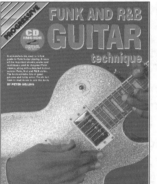

PROGRESSIVE BLUES GUITAR SOLOS
INTERMEDIATE TO ADVANCED

Contains a great selection of Blues solos in a variety of styles reflecting the whole history of the Blues tradition from early Delta Blues to contemporary Blues Rock. Demonstrates various methods of creating solos along with sections on vocal style phrasing, call and response, developing a theme, dynamics and the use of space. Many of the solos are written in the styles of Blues legends like Muddy Waters, John Lee Hooker, BB, Albert and Freddy King, Buddy Guy, Albert Collins, Peter Green, Magic Sam, Otis Rush, Eric Clapton and Stevie Ray Vaughan.

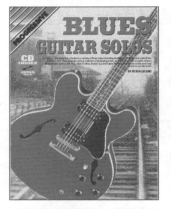

PROGRESSIVE FUNK AND R&B GUITAR TECHNIQUE
INTERMEDIATE TO ADVANCED

Covers a range of exciting chord sounds essential to Funk, along with the Dorian and Mixolydian modes and the use of harmonic intervals such as 6ths, 3rds, 4ths, octaves and tritones. Also features a thorough study of rhythms and right hand techniques such as percussive strumming and string muting. A range of Funk styles are examined, as well as some great Soul and R&B sounds.

PROGRESSIVE GUITAR CHORDS
FOR BEGINNER TO ADVANCED GUITARISTS

Shows you every useful chord shape in every key. An open chord section for beginners contains the simplest and most widely used chord shapes in all keys. A bar chord section for the semi-advanced player who will need a thorough knowledge of bar chord shapes in all positions. A section for the advanced player listing the moveable shapes for chords widely used by Jazz guitarists. Other sections contain important music theory for the guitarist including scales, keys and chord construction.

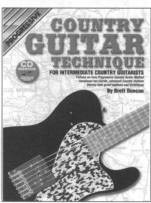

PROGRESSIVE COUNTRY GUITAR TECHNIQUE
FOR INTERMEDIATE GUITARISTS

This book continues on from *Progressive Country Guitar Method*. More basic chords are covered such as Major Sixth, Minor Seventh, Major Seventh, Augmented and Diminished. This book introduces triplet rhythms, rhythm rests and staccato strumming. The most common Bar chords are also studied and several Country lead guitar patterns and techniques are featured.